PRESSURE POINTS

Where Cultural Norms Meet Biblical Truth

FREDDY
Thank you for your leadership and your faithfulness,

Gregg T. Johnson

COPYRIGHT © 2020
Gregg T. Johnson

All rights reserved. No part of this book may be reproduced, stored in a retrieval system, or transmitted in any form or by any means—electronic, mechanical, photocopy, recording, or any other—except for brief quotations in printed reviews, without the prior permission of Gregg Johnson

All scripture quotations are taken from The Holy Bible, New King James Version, Copyright © 1982 by Thomas Nelson, Inc.
(unless otherwise noted)

ISBN 978-0-9741036-8-6

April 1, 2020

A special thank you to
Heather Chapdelaine and Pastor Linda Schreck
For proofreading and editing

Additional copies are available by contacting:

The Mission Church
4101 Rt. 52, Holmes NY 12531, USA
www.missionchurch.com

A portion of the proceeds goes to equipping Christian Leaders around the world.

Published by Global Leadership Training
Holmes, New York, USA

Printed in the United States by Morris Publishing®
3212 East Highway 30
Kearney, NE 68847
1-800-650-7888

TABLE OF CONTENTS

Foreword by Dr. Michael Brown	5
Preface to Pressure Points	9
Being Salt in a Culture of Decay	15
Different Gospel, Same Old Lies	25
Morality and Truth	43
Creation and the Origin of Man	61
The Sanctity of Human Life	77
Promiscuity and Marriage	97
Homosexuality and Gender	111
Speak the Truth, Even if Your Voice Shakes	127
A Call for Compassionate Confrontation	143
Introduction to Appendices	149
Appendix I: Introduction to Resolution	151
Appendix II: Resolution on Marriage, Sexuality and Sanctity of Life	153
Endnotes	158
About the Author	160

Pressure Points

FOREWORD

Dr. Michael L. Brown
Host of the Line of Fire Radio Broadcast
President of FIRE School of Ministry (AskDrBrown.org)

For many years I have said that I am not so much concerned about the presence of darkness in our society as much as with the absence of light. Darkness will always be dark, by nature. It is the light that must shine.

In this important book, Pastor Gregg Johnson calls on us—the people of God, the Church, and leaders in particular—to fulfill our God-given role as salt and light. We must get the Lord's heart, full of compassion, love, and truth, and we must stand up and speak up. Otherwise, the world will collapse around us. How ironic that the very world that hates us in reality so desperately needs us!

What blesses me most about this book is that it is written by a pastor, since all too often, pastors in America fall short here. They don't want to offend their congregants. They don't want to have a bad reputation in the community. They don't want to lose their best tithers. They don't want to fall out of favor with their boards or their denominational leaders. But, as Pastor Gregg has written, "Being a pastor means not worrying about who might be offended when we speak the truth; instead, it's worrying about who will continue being deceived if we don't."

Back in 2014, Christian pollster George Barna was on American Family Radio discussing the results of his latest survey. He explained that, "What we're finding is that when we ask [pastors] about all the key issues of the day, [90 percent of them are] telling us, 'Yes, the Bible speaks to every one of these issues.' Then we ask them: 'Well, are you teaching your people what the Bible says about those issues?' and the numbers drop…to less than 10 percent of pastors who say they will speak to it."

What a stinging indictment. These pastors agreed that the Bible addressed all the key issues of the day, yet less than 10 percent of them were willing to use the Bible to address these issues. And what, exactly, held them back from addressing controversial issues from the pulpit, including, "societal, moral and political issues"? According to Barna, "There are five factors that the vast majority of pastors turn to: attendance, giving, number of programs, number of staff, and square footage."

He continued: "What I'm suggesting is [those pastors] won't probably get involved in politics because it's very controversial. Controversy keeps people from being in the seats, controversy keeps people from giving money, from attending programs."

I wonder how we will feel on the day we stand before God and give account, especially as pastors and leaders. Will we be able to look into the Lord's eyes and say, "But I didn't want to hurt people's feelings"? Or, will we "Lord, I was afraid that our finances would dry up if I obeyed you"? Or, "Jesus, I was more concerned with my reputation than with Yours"? In the biting words of the Methodist preacher W. E. Sangster, "How shall I feel at the Judgment, if multitudes of missed opportunities pass before me in full review, and all my excuses prove to be disguises of my cowardice and pride?"

As a pastor, you might say, "But it's not always so easy. If our budget goes down, we can't feed needy children in our neighborhood. How does the Lord feel about that? Or what if we have to cut support for a missionary overseas? What then? Was it really worth the controversy? And if we get associated with controversial political issues, we will alienate the very people we want to reach. Isn't it best that we avoid the hot-button issues and major on the majors?"

Those are all valid points, and that's why you are reading this book. As a pastor, Gregg Johnson understands the challenges and is sensitive to the pressures. He cares about God and he cares about people. And he will be a wise guide to help you navigate these difficult waters, enabling you to identify when cowardice disguises itself as wisdom and when the fear of man disguises itself as compassion. Then, being armed with the truth and with a heart full of love, you can serve as a faithful shepherd of the flock and a loyal servant of the Lord.

Pastor Gregg quotes Maggie Kuhn, who said, "Speak the truth, even if your voice shakes." In fact, he devotes a whole chapter to this subject, reminding all of us our need for the Lord's sustaining power. In your weakness, you can find His strength. And you will find Pastor Gregg's thinking to be clear, incisive, and scriptural. On page after page (really, in sentence after sentence), I found myself giving a hearty "Amen!" Your spirit will be stirred as you read.

The bottom line is that God has appointed us to be His witnesses, and our people live in the midst of a fallen, messed up world. If we don't speak, if we don't provide answers, if we don't give moral guidance, if we don't set an example, our people will fall into despair and confusion. As I noted in a video commentary titled, "Why Don't More Pastors Speak Out?", our kids and grandkids must deal with questions about abortion, about drug use, about suicide, about sexuality, about the meaning of gender. These issues are directly affecting them and their friends. How can we who are leaders not provide solid answers for them? How can we not help equip their parents and teachers? Isn't this also part of our role as shepherds and leaders?

Truly, Gregg Johnson writes with the passion of a prophet and the practicality of a pastor, exposing modern variations of the gospel (which are really not the gospel at all), addressing our pervasive moral relativism, exposing the dangers of hyper-grace, pointing to our divinely created purpose, and outlining the great cultural issues of the day, from abortion to promiscuity and from homosexuality to transgenderism. The fact that you now hold this book in your hands (or own it in digital form) means that you are ready to be part of the solution.

And so, I speak to you as a fellow leader in the Body: If not you, then who? And if not now, then when? Together in the Lord, empowered by His Spirit, we can make a lasting difference. So, arise and shine! You were called and appointed for such a time as this.

Pressure Points

PREFACE TO PRESSURE POINTS

Satan is not fighting churches, he's joining them. He does more harm by sowing tares than pulling up wheat.
- Vance Havner

The kingdom of heaven is like a man who sowed good seed in his field; but while men slept, his enemy came and sowed tares among the wheat and went his way."
- Matthew 13:24-25

It's not a culture war that we are engaged in, it's a spiritual war. The enemies we face are not trying to win political debates, they are trying to establish strongholds of deception that resist the truth of God and imprison us in lies. It's not just about same-sex marriage, abortion or transgenderism, it's about creating a worldview that denies the very existence of God and rejects the need for a Savior. It's the age-old story of man being told, "Hath God said?" and embracing a worldview that rejects the authority of the Creator.

Unfortunately, the intensity of this spiritual battle has increased significantly. By manipulating culture and preying upon the empty souls of lost and broken people, the god of this world has established strongholds to propagate his lies that hold the masses in deception. Our society has become a quagmire of "arguments and every high thing that exalts itself against the knowledge of God" (2 Corinthians 10:5). Again, it's not simply about debates over morality, it's about establishing a cultural resentment against God's revealed truth and fixing a societal bulwark of rebellion against His authority. It's in this morass of delusion that the enemy blinds souls to truth and holds them captive to his will. Today, tragically, millions upon millions are broken and suffering because they lack the benefit of a biblical, Christ-centered worldview. They have no truth to set them free.

Perhaps even more disturbing is that those who have the truth—the people of God, His church, the Body of Christ—are not forthright concerning it. Instead of speaking truth clearly and persuasively, we champion tolerance and accommodate society's godlessness. Somehow, we believe it's the way to win the world to Christ: don't offend them by talking about man's sin and the need for repentance, befriend them by talking about God's love and offer of acceptance. Unfortunately, by taking this approach, we give the world a false hope and make peace with the immorality that has destroyed countless lives. Even more, the immorality we've permitted in the name of tolerance has become a force to inform the very culture of the church. Issues such as abortion, homosexuality, cohabitation and premarital sex are no longer taboo for Christians, in many circles, these are quite the norm.

This is why I wrote *Pressure Points*. In this climate of growing indifference in leadership, not only has the church become ineffective in its ability to influence culture, the culture is influencing and reshaping the church. Certain issues have come to the forefront as society is pressuring the church to accept as normal what the Bible clearly identifies as sin. This should not be happening. The church exists to be salt and light in the world by glorifying God and declaring truth. We should be influencing the world, not the reverse. Therefore, it has become necessary for church leaders to be more intentional; we must call out specific issues that are infiltrating the church, deceiving believers and preventing Christians from discerning a delusion.

There are several pressure points that are of concern today: homosexuality and same-sex marriage, transgenderism and sexual identity, cohabitation and promiscuity, moral relativism and biblical illiteracy, and abortion and the sanctity of life. These issues have become contentious topics for the church as society is urging us to accept its values and embrace those who defiantly practice them. They are sinful lifestyles that the church is being pressured to accept as Christian norms. And those Christians or churches that dare to resist this pressure are branded as bigoted and evil and are marginalized as extremists who threaten society. In fact, it is likely that legislation will ensue to further restrict religious freedom in an attempt to force the church's compliance.

Sadly, many believers, churches and denominations have acquiesced to this pressure and embraced these practices in defiance of scripture. The latest example is, as of the writing of this book, the anticipated split of the United Methodist Church into two branches, one that affirms biblical marriage and one that celebrates homosexual unions. With over 12 million members, the UMC is the largest denomination within the wider Methodist movement of approximately 80 million people worldwide and is among the largest protestant denominations in the United States. This signifies a huge shift in the church—one that we cannot ignore. What began as tolerance, evolved into acceptance and has now become an established norm. The culture of this world is taking root in the church and soon the two will be indistinguishable. This is why it is necessary for the church to affirm its biblically held positions and declare its fidelity to the canon of scripture.

This is especially true as the evangelical church continues to grow and more people join as voting members to determine church policy and doctrine. It is likely that some newcomers seeking membership may not be entirely clear on biblical standards regarding homosexuality, same-sex marriage, transgenderism, cohabitation, and abortion. If left unchecked, this may result in a future membership populated with individuals who approve of these practices, even tacitly. The outcome could be a next generation of members that may resist and oppose future attempts to affirm biblical positions on these cultural issues. At best, this could become a split in the church similar to the UMC; at worst, it could result in a complete takeover of specific churches by heretical factions.

Clarity on these issues needs to become a part of the church's culture and assimilation processes. To remain ambiguous is to ignore Jesus' warning to sleeping leaders who allowed tares to be sown among the wheat (Matthew 13:24-30). Specifically, there should be instruction provided that explains biblical positions in a clear and compassionate way. Addressing these issues proactively may bring controversy and might even discourage some people from joining the church in membership; however, if leaders do not address them now, the controversial nature will only become more hostile as time progresses. The tares will grow and become part of the crop; pulling them apart will be difficult, if not impossible. Now is the time to act, rather than later.

In the church where I pastor, we took steps to address these issues proactively and prevent the sowing of tares among the wheat. I preached a series of messages to provide biblical clarity on the above-stated pressure points. It was a series that strengthened the unity of our church while promoting a greater love for the Word of God. People appreciated the clarity and explanations and felt empowered to stand firm in the cultural confusion of today. Each chapter of this book represents a particular topic that was addressed during this series. If you're a pastor, I encourage you to use this material to educate your church as well. If you are a Bible study leader or a homegroup facilitator, this could be a great resource to take your group into a deeper understanding of scripture. If you're not in leadership, and simply have a concern for the trends of the church, may you be challenged and empowered to stand firm in a climate of concession and compromise.

Finally, at the conclusion of the series, our church membership was presented with a resolution to codify our positions on these issues as "significant religious beliefs" in our church constitution and bylaws. I am grateful to the Alliance Defending Freedom (ADF) for their assistance in developing the language for the resolution and guidance in presenting it to our membership. ADF is an alliance of more than 3,400 attorneys to assist churches and individuals in defending religious liberty in America and around the world. The resolution we adopted is provided in the appendix of this book. Please feel free to use it as a template for your church as well.

Pressure Points

Pressure Points

introduction
BEING SALT IN A CULTURE OF DECAY

Don't be upset at the meat that putrefies. It's just doing what meat does naturally—it rots and decays. Instead, be upset at the salt for not preserving it.

You are the salt of the earth; but if the salt loses its flavor, how shall it be seasoned? It is then good for nothing but to be thrown out and trampled underfoot by men. - Matthew 5:13

The church is losing its voice in a day when it desperately needs to be heard.

In twenty-first-century western culture, truth has become a quagmire of political correctness and moral relativism. Everyone does what is right in their own sight. Any reference to an authoritative standard of right and wrong is mocked as an antiquated relic from a barbaric, unenlightened past. Tolerance of depravity is the new virtue and one's signaled awareness of what is politically correct awards them the title of being "woke."

What is most concerning, however, is not the darkened immorality of the world; that's to be expected. More concerning is the apparent neutrality of the church regarding this immorality. Talk to most Christians today about the moral issues which concern them, and you will hear about sex trafficking, racial injustice, and poverty—the "woke issues" of today. But mention such things as transgenderism, evolution, abortion and homosexuality, topics that draw criticism and controversy, and those same Christians have little to say. In fact, many believers avoid these matters entirely.

This is especially true among church leaders. Many pastors and Christian influencers will champion causes to alleviate hunger or confront slavery in third world countries, but when asked about abortion or same-sex marriage, they'll say "That's a personal matter I only discuss with individuals in private." Some appear so neutral on the issues that their silence suggests tacit approval. Others offer explanations so slippery they border on heresy. In any case, such a lack of clarity is a betrayal of truth and is complicit with the immorality holding our society prisoner. Like a parent who enables her child's addiction by refusing to confront him, the church has enabled the decline of western culture by refusing to be a voice of clarity and truth.

Undoubtedly, there will be those who ask, "Why should the church be vocal on social issues? Isn't that 'moralism?' Shouldn't preachers just preach the gospel and focus on religious things like prayer and worship? Shouldn't Christians be known by 'what they are for' and not 'for what they are against?'" While such statements make cute clichés and provide cover from controversy, they do not provide clarity to a world held prisoner to delusion and lies. Furthermore, if your "gospel" does not compel you to speak truth in the presence of lies, then your gospel is different from the biblical gospel.

Charles Colson wrote: "We need prayer, Bible study, worship, fellowship, and witnessing. But if we focus exclusively on these disciplines – and if in the process we ignore our responsibility to redeem the surrounding culture – our Christianity will remain privatized and marginalized. Turning our backs on the culture is a betrayal of our biblical mandate and our own heritage because it denies God's sovereignty over all of life."[1]

To what "biblical mandate" is Colson referring? The mandate to live as salt and light in this world.

THE MANDATE OF SALT AND LIGHT

The metaphors of salt and light give us a proper perspective of Jesus' expectation regarding His followers' influence on culture. Salt is a preservative that prevents decay in meat that would otherwise rot, and light is an element that dispels darkness wherever it is present. Since the earliest days of Christianity, the church, as salt and light, has confronted the decay and darkness of society—

not merely to champion what Christians "are for," but to also define what the Word of God "is against." It's by clearly declaring truth that the Word of God comes alive and the Holy Spirit is released to "convict the world of sin, and of righteousness, and of judgment" (John 16:8).

It is also by speaking to the issues of culture that the church maintains its relevant voice. We should not make the mistake of thinking that "relevance" is simply being stylish and trendy. While it is essential that churches contextualize the message and speak the language of the surrounding culture, we must remember that no soul was ever set free because a church was "cool." It's the truth that sets free and the truth is always relevant. When the church raises its voice with boldness, clarity and divinely enabled wisdom, it remains part of the conversation, and the world will be provoked to listen. If, however, we stay silent on controversial issues in order to appear non-threatening and culturally compatible, we reinforce the notion that faith is personal, not public. We will marginalize ourselves through self-invoked silence, and the salt will be good for nothing but to be thrown out and trampled underfoot by men (Matt. 5:13).

THE CHURCH AS SALT IN HISTORY

Speaking truth to culture is not new to the church. In fact, the role of salt and light in society has been part of the church's mission since Jesus commanded us to "Go into all the world" (Mark 16:15).

When the cultural norm of third-century Rome allowed sick people to die in streets, it was the church in 325 AD, at the Council of Nicaea, that called for the creation of hospitals in every region a bishop served. When the cultural norm in the 4th century was to discard disabled infants, it was the church that established the first orphanages. In the 18th century, when the poor and underprivileged were abandoned, it was the church that developed poorhouses to care for them. During the missionary expansion of the 1700s and beyond, it was Christian missionaries that introduced public education and literacy around the world to those they served.

Throughout history, it was the church that challenged culture and was a catalyst for change. It was the church that opposed the abuse of power in monarchies and the corruption in its own papal system. It was the church that fought to improve conditions for the impoverished, homeless, disabled, and labored to improve circumstances in prisons. It was the church during the Industrial Revolution that fought for improved working environments for factory workers and confronted the abuse of children forced to labor in those harsh situations.

When slavery was an international industry fueling national economies, it was the church who opposed it, spoke out against it, and created a movement to end it. In England, an evangelical Christian named William Wilberforce, a member of the British parliament, led the movement to end slavery in England and all British colonies. In the United States, it was the church—specifically the Baptists, Presbyterians, Quakers, and Methodists—who forced the hand of the abolition of slavery. Two-thirds of the abolitionist's society of 1835 were ministers of the gospel. Leading members of the Underground Railroad were devout Quakers. Abraham Lincoln was a sincere Christian who loved the Bible. In fact, so powerful was the influence of Christianity against slavery, that some historians believe there would have never been a Civil War to free the slaves without the instigation of the church.

When Women's Suffrage was fighting for the right of women to vote, many churches and Christian leaders were vocal in their support of the cause. Although clergymen on both sides of the issue used biblical arguments to bolster their position, many denominations, including Methodists, Presbyterians, and Catholics, played a key role in the passage of the 19th Amendment.

In Nazi Germany, in the 1930s and 1940s, church leaders like Dietrich Bonhoeffer openly opposed Adolf Hitler's culture of anti-Semitism and boldly resisted his policies to euthanize the Jews. Bonhoeffer's determination to be salt and light in Germany eventually landed him in Buchenwald and then the Flossenbürg concentration camp. On April 9, 1945, he was hanged. For what? He refused to be silent, believing that his silence would be complicit with a culture turned rotten.

In the United States, in the 1960s, a young preacher named Dr. Martin Luther King, Jr. supported by networks of churches and bishops, organized the struggle for civil rights. The church stood by its leaders through brutal opposition, even after Dr. King's assassination. In Alabama, The African Methodist Episcopal Church played a pivotal role, conducting marches which led to the passage of the 1965 Voting Rights Act. Even today, churches in African American communities continue to challenge culture by improving urban communities with persistent diligence and amazing faith.

Thankfully, leaders such as Wilberforce, Bonhoeffer, and King did not remain silent to avoid offending their audience. They risked their popularity. They risked their ministries. They risked their very lives for the cause of truth and morality. Today we celebrate them as heroes for taking a stand, making their positions clear and putting themselves at odds with great multitudes of people who advocated for evils they opposed.

The point is clear: Jesus commanded His church to be salt and light in society. We exist under a mandate to be agents of influence in culture. As salt prevents decay and light dispels darkness, we are to rise with a clear voice, speaking truth, taking action and offering solutions. It is the church's mandate to confront the cultural confusion and delusion that has so many in its grip.

In 21st century American society, this mandate continues. Not only is there concern over the broad spectrum of immorality in pop culture, but there is also concern that this immorality is taking root in a church that has grown silent. External pressure from the media, journalism, and politics have persuaded many in Christendom to accept as normal what the Bible clearly identifies as sin. Right before our eyes, antibiblical and ungodly standards are infiltrating the church as many Christians lose their ability to discern the corruption.

It is time for a robust response. If the church truly exists to be salt in the earth and light in the world, it is essential for Christ-followers, church leaders and denominational heads to champion a biblical worldview. If we do not speak up and raise our voices openly, we will be sidelined altogether. If we continue on this path to reframe cultural issues merely as personal conversations and avoid answering the difficult questions in the public square, the church will lose its influence entirely. We will reinforce the notion that Biblical truth should be relegated to the margins of the cultural conversation only to be addressed as personal, privatized matters of conscience.

PRESSURE POINTS

There are several issues of particular concern today: abortion, homosexuality, transgenderism, cohabitation, sexual promiscuity, naturalism, the origin of man and an impotent, modernized gospel. These issues stand out because they have become cultural pressure points within the church. Society is forcefully demanding churches to approve and accept immoral practices as normal, healthy lifestyle choices. And this pressure is relentless.

Just listen to the criticism coming from pop-culture, academia, professional sports, journalism, politics, and even some religious groups. Intense pressure is being put on the church to accept blatantly sinful practices as Christian norms. Sadly, many believers, churches and denominations have acquiesced in defiance of scripture. More and more, we are hearing of churches that assimilate and ordain homosexuals, marry same-sex couples, advocate for abortion rights, encourage transgenderism, and propagate a naturalistic worldview.

More notably, many Christians who have achieved prominence in pop culture are likely to water-down biblical truth in order to preserve their popularity and influence. Appearing on mainstream talk shows or trendy podcasts, they are bold concerning the palatable aspects of the gospel but are reluctant to address matters of morality and ethics. If they do address moral issues, they usually target socially acceptable ones like world hunger, poverty, and human trafficking; hardly ever will they speak out against homosexuality, transgenderism, sexual purity or abortion. In many cases, their ambiguity or silence, signal an approval of immorality and serve only to advance the deception that holds so many in its grip.

While many "leaders" are weak in their response, others have become bold advocates of the heresy. This is especially true of same-sex marriage issues and the acceptance of LGBTQ lifestyles. Such advocates include the Reform and Conservative Jewish movements, the Unitarian Universalist Association, the United Church of Christ, and the Episcopal Church who now solemnizes same-sex marriage ceremonies after approving a new definition of marriage. As well, the Presbyterian Church (U.S.A.) has recently joined this movement to advocate for homosexuality by voting to sanction gay marriages.

It's become known in our culture as "Progressive Christianity," a movement of denominations and churches that promote social justice and "cultural salvation" in the name of Christ. Although it sounds decent, Progressive Christianity rejects the doctrine of the inerrancy of Scripture and prides itself on questioning the traditional absolutes of faith and morality. This explains why these denominations readily affirm marriage rights for same-sex couples and regard moral relativism as a virtue. Once a denomination untethers itself from the authority of God's Word, anything goes. There is no standard, there are no absolutes, everyone is free to do what is right in their own sight.

As the church continues this decline, the light dims, the salt loses its flavor, and it affects the cultural consciousness. Pastors and church leaders who are ambiguous regarding truth and error allow deception to rise unabated. As a result, culture darkens and morality decays while individuals and families are encouraged to find their own truth apart from biblical authority. According to a recent Pew Research Center survey, most mainline Protestants (66 percent) now support same-sex marriage, as do a similar share of Catholics (61%). Furthermore, about four-in-ten of those who attend church once a week (39 percent) support same-sex marriage, compared with 66 percent who attend a few times a year.[2] Tragically, it seems we are experiencing the "Great Falling Away" that Paul prophesied in 1 Timothy 4:1-2: "Now the Spirit expressly says that in latter times some will depart from the faith, giving heed to deceiving spirits and doctrines of demons, speaking lies in hypocrisy, having their own conscience seared with a hot iron."

Clearly, the culture of this world is taking root in the church and soon the two will be indistinguishable. Today's Christians desperately need to affirm their biblically held ideals and declare fidelity to the canon of scripture. This is especially true as it relates to these cultural pressure points. Neutrality is no longer an option. Silence is no longer a strategy. The Body of Christ must reclaim its voice in the world as an authority defining right from wrong, light from darkness, and life from death. Salt is needed. We must remove any ambiguity regarding God's Word and clearly articulate His good, perfect and acceptable will for mankind.

RELEVANCE WITHOUT COMPROMISE

Obviously, if the church's message is to be heard, believers must be culturally sensitive and speak the language people understand. We must be relevant. Our means and methods must be familiar and relate well to those we are trying to reach, or we'll never influence them. But our pursuit of relevance should never be a reason for compromise or an excuse for silence. As we speak to the issues of culture, we must be careful not to dilute God's Word or make peace with the attitudes and immorality that have destroyed countless lives. People are searching for answers, and the answers we give must be the whole gospel and not merely the palatable parts.

Equally important is our motive of love. Individual believers and churches should reach out in genuine concern and compassion to those bound in sin. Antagonists who contend against the truth should be met with respect and engaged with grace, kindness, and wisdom. They should not be ostracized, ridiculed or disdained. Our words and actions, demonstrated in love, should make it impossible for critics to brand us as bigots, haters or homophobes. But our motive of love should never be an excuse for avoiding the difficult truths. Our message must be clear; it must have the capacity to cut the heart, pierce the soul, generate conviction and produce repentance through the power of the Holy Spirit. This world needs more than intellectual arguments that win debates, it needs Spirit-led, truth-empowered men and women of God who win converts and make disciples.

Such men and women must be completely sold out to the purposes of God. They must have the passion to speak like a prophet, lead like an apostle, and love like a pastor. They cannot be concerned about attracting crowds and building a brand, but need the uncompromising character of John the Baptist, the flint-hard countenance of Ezekiel, and the stalwart courage of Elijah.

This is my desire as you read these pages. I hope you will be inspired to "Preach the word...in season and out of season [and to] convince, rebuke, exhort, with all longsuffering and teaching" (2 Timothy 4:2). I hope they will equip you with a template to address these pressure points in an effective and reasonable manner. And while I am certain that better minds than mine and far more capable preachers than me could do a far superior job in presenting this material, I simply hope to spark a fire. I pray that you will be inspired to be a voice to our generation and declare the truth of God's Word set against the pressure points of this world, to expose deception, bring conviction and set people free through the power of God.

Pressure Points

one
DIFFERENT GOSPEL, SAME OLD LIES

Being a pastor means not worrying about who might be offended when we speak the truth; instead, it's worrying about who will continue being deceived if we don't.

Preach the word! For the time will come when they will not endure sound doctrine, but according to their own desires, because they have itching ears, they will heap up for themselves teachers. - Timothy 4:2-3

Since the beginning of Christianity, church leaders have had concerns about cultural influences that would pervert the gospel. In Galatia, Paul "marveled" that so many had been easily drawn into a "different gospel" and wrote, "There are some who trouble you and want to pervert the gospel of Christ. But even if we, or an angel from heaven, preach any other gospel to you than what we have preached to you, let him be accursed" (Galatians 1:7-8). In Corinth, Paul offered an even stronger warning: "For if he who comes preaches another Jesus whom we have not preached, or if you receive a different spirit which you have not received, or a different gospel which you have not accepted—you may well put up with it!" (2 Corinthians 11:4). He continues: "For such are false apostles, deceitful workers, transforming themselves into apostles of Christ. And no wonder! For Satan himself transforms himself into an angel of light" (2 Corinthians 11:13-14).

These admonitions were a reoccurring theme in Paul's ministry. In Acts 20, he warned the elders of Ephesus: "Take heed to yourselves and to all the flock, among which the Holy Spirit has made you overseers, to shepherd the church of God which He purchased with His own blood. For I know this, that after my departure savage wolves will come in among you, not sparing the flock. Also, from among yourselves men will rise up, speaking perverse things, to draw away the disciples after themselves" (Acts 20:28-30).

The warnings of Paul were not lost on the early church. The apostle anticipated a future in which church culture would be so influenced by the world that believers would prefer error more than truth. "For the time will come when they will not endure sound doctrine, but according to their own desires, because they have itching ears, they will heap up for themselves teachers; and they will turn their ears away from the truth, and be turned aside to fables" (2 Timothy 4:3-4). He then offers insight into what this may look like: "Now the Spirit expressly says that in latter times some will depart from the faith, giving heed to deceiving spirits and doctrines of demons, speaking lies in hypocrisy, having their own conscience seared with a hot iron…" (1 Timothy 4:1-2). Paul is even more descriptive in 2 Timothy 3:1-5 when he says, "In the last days perilous times will come: For men will be lovers of themselves, lovers of money, boasters, proud, blasphemers, disobedient to parents, unthankful, unholy, unloving, unforgiving, slanderers, without self-control, brutal, despisers of good, traitors, headstrong, haughty, lovers of pleasure rather than lovers of God, having a form of godliness but denying its power. And from such people turn away!"

The cautions are clear. A time is coming when those who have a form of the gospel, will deny the power of that gospel having diluted it with their love of the world. It's an era when some in the church will so conform to the culture that they will lose their distinction from it—and even become advocates for it. It will be a season when leaders must "contend earnestly for the faith once delivered to the saints" (Jude 1:3). And it's why Paul exhorted Timothy and all preachers who would follow: "Preach the word! Be ready in season and out of season. Convince, rebuke, exhort, with all longsuffering and teaching" (2 Timothy 4:1-2).

PREACH THE WORD

In an age of false teachers and a diluted gospel, truth is what's needed most. Truth must be spoken. It must be proclaimed. Whenever a lie is told and people are deceived, only truth can pierce the delusion. It must be truth that is undiluted, uncompromised, unapologetic and clear. Yes, it must be spoken with love and grace—but it must be spoken. Jesus said, "You shall know the truth, and the truth shall make you free" (John 8:31-32).

But for the truth to be known, it must be told—and for the truth to be told, it requires a truth-teller. Someone must be willing to speak it. Unfortunately, many are reluctant to do so, believing it's better to stay quiet: "If we offend people, we can't win them. If we speak out, we could drive them away." As a result, leaders remain silent on the issues of the day, convincing themselves that silence is wisdom and a muted message is love and grace.

But silence is not always wisdom, nor should it be mistaken for love and grace. In a day when the unborn are slaughtered in the name of health care, children are mutilated under the guise of gender correction and delusion is brazenly militant, silence can be cowardice. Mahatma Ghandi said, "Silence becomes cowardice when occasion demands speaking out the whole truth and acting accordingly." Alexandr Solzhenitsyn said, "The simple step of a courageous individual is not to take part in the lie. One word of truth outweighs the world." Maggie Kuhn said, "Speak the truth, even if your voice shakes." As pastors we should be less worried about those who are offended when we speak the truth, and more worried about those who will continue being deceived if we don't.

Indeed, how one speaks the truth is crucial to the message. The truth-teller needs discretion. Standing on a table and shouting at your co-workers is probably not the right approach, neither is using a bullhorn on a street corner the best way to preach the gospel. What we say and how we say it is critical—but speak we must. High-profile preachers, who have a platform but refuse to speak truth to a culture of lies, are wasting their influence. Pastors who neglect to comment regarding issues of the day are failing their generation. Will people disagree? Sure. Will some be offended? Probably. Will members leave the church? Quite possibly. But do we hold back? Do we mute our message? Do we obfuscate the truth in hopes that our listeners will friend us and be converted by our mere eloquence? Do we really think that such an approach will produce true and lasting repentance?

I agree that truth must be spoken with love and grace. But I am concerned that we have taken this to mean that truth cannot be spoken at all—that if our truth offends someone, then we aren't loving them. This is nonsense. Leaders who never offend anyone are not leading. Leadership confronts. Leadership challenges. Leadership pulls people. It doesn't take people where they want to go, it pushes them where they need to go.

This generation has too many pastors who are pretenders. They are not leading. They are placating. Their messages soothe and comfort, but have no capacity to convict of sin and produce repentance. Their churches are full, their altars are full, their worship concerts are full—but full of what? If a sin-hardened soul can sit in our services, enjoy the sermons and never be confronted by the truth of God's Word, something is wrong. If a person who rejects the authority of scripture because it contradicts their "lifestyle" can feel comforted in our worship concerts because the music is so soothing—what have we accomplished? If church members are cohabiting without marriage, aborting their babies, committing sodomy, mutilating their children's gender, and never feel conviction, shame on us. We have failed. I am not saying we should berate, condemn or scold our people. I am saying we should simply preach the gospel—all of it.

If you are a typical church member, take note. If your "pastor" never confronts your idols or challenges your sin—if he only affirms you as you are—he's not being a pastor. Pastoral leadership shouldn't just celebrate who you are, it should call you into the likeness of Christ, and force you to confront your rebellious ways. Church members who want pastors to only give them happy thoughts and uplifting homilies are no different than terminal patients seeking doctors who only give positive medical reports. Such doctors—and pastors—are worthless.

THE GOSPEL DEFINED

Before addressing the issues that are diluting the gospel today, we must first understand exactly what the gospel is. Simply stated, the gospel is the good news that we are rescued from God's wrath through Jesus Christ the Lord. From this definition, we find four truths that define it from a biblical foundation.

First, The Gospel is the Good News that We are Rescued. The word "gospel" means "good news. It comes from the Greek word "euangelion" which occurs over 130 times in the New Testament (including derivatives). It conveys the idea of announcing news that brings hope and joy to those who need it.

Tim Keller describes the gospel as "news of something that has happened to rescue and deliver people from peril."[1] It is news about our rescue. It's the message that God has done something for us, and offers something to us, which we are invited to receive.

Paul the Apostle wrote, "I am not ashamed of the gospel of Christ, for it is the power of God to salvation for everyone who believes, for the Jew first and also for the Greek" (Romans 1:16). According to Paul, this good news is more than mere happy thoughts to make us feel better, it is a proclamation of eternal salvation for every man, woman, and child who needs to be rescued.

But rescued from what? From what danger do we need to be saved? The Bible provides a clear and obvious answer: we need to be rescued from the wrath of God.

Second, The Gospel is the Good News that We are Rescued from God's Wrath. R.C. Sproul said, "The gospel is only good news when we understand the bad news." Before we can truly appreciate the gospel, we must understand why we need it. As explained by the Apostle Paul in Romans chapter one, all mankind is born in sin, rebellious by nature, guilty before God and destined to eternal punishment.

God did not create us this way. He created us in His own perfect image (Genesis 1:27). However, with that reflection of Himself, God gave us the ability to choose. Rather than preprogrammed human units wired to obey, the Creator wanted our obedience to be a choice, born out of love for Him. Tragically, mankind used that power of choice to rebel and fell into sin. Now,

God's perfect creation is broken—a brokenness that poisons every human soul (Romans 5:12).

The bad news for us lies in the fact that God is just—and because He is just, He must punish sin. This means every person, because all have sinned, is under the condemnation of God (John 3:18). Most people avoid this truth, focusing only on the love of God, but any description of God that solely depicts His love is incomplete. He is also "just." In fact, He is a Just Judge, compelled by His just nature, to condemn sinners (Genesis 18:25). This is why Romans 12:19 reminds us, "Vengeance is mine, says the Lord, I will repay." And Hebrews 9:27 says "It is appointed unto man to die once, but after this, the judgment."

It is not a popular message, but it's the truth on which the gospel rests. It's the bad news that provides context for the good news: God's wrath awaits the sinner. It's why Jesus said, "Fear Him who is able to destroy both soul and body in Hell (Matthew 10:28); and John wrote, "The smoke of their torment ascends forever and ever."

This is why it's called the gospel—the good news. Despite our sin, guilt and imminent demise, God loves us and provides a rescue.

Third, The Gospel is the Good News that We are Rescued from God's Wrath through Jesus Christ. John 3:16 is one of the greatest verses in the Bible: "For God so loved the world that He gave His only begotten Son, that whoever believes in Him should not perish but have everlasting life." In this scripture, we see both the love of God and the justice of God satisfied through the Son, Jesus Christ.

2 Corinthians 5:21 says, "He made Him who knew no sin to be sin for us, that we might become the righteousness of God in Him." God the Son became man so He could identify with man in his lost estate. Although sinless, Jesus became a vicarious atonement for the guilt of man on the cross. Isaiah 53:6 says "The Lord laid on Him the iniquity of us all." He bore the wrath of God for us. Every lash that tore His flesh, each nail that pierced his body, the crown of thorns upon His brow, was punishment meant for us. He paid the price we should have paid. He died the death we

should have died.

Herein lies the great truth of the incarnation: by becoming man, Jesus could represent mankind. By remaining God, He could pay the ransom for mankind. The worth of His blood, the infinite value of his divine life, could purchase the rescue for every man, woman, and child ever born. He is that Lamb of God who takes away the sins of the world.

There are conditions, however. This salvation is not automatically applied to every guilty soul. Romans 10:9-10 says, "If you confess with your mouth the Lord Jesus and believe in your heart that God has raised Him from the dead, you will be saved. For with the heart one believes unto righteousness, and with the mouth confession is made unto salvation." Acts 2:38 records Peter's words to three thousand people who responded on the Day of Pentecost: "Repent, and let every one of you be baptized in the name of Jesus Christ for the remission of sins; and you shall receive the gift of the Holy Spirit."

Scripture tells us each person must make a choice to embrace this act of divine redemption. Every individual must accept the grace that God offers. It requires trust in the atoning work of Christ, repentance from the rebellion of man that drove Jesus to the cross, and submission to Him as Lord of one's life.

Fourth, The Gospel is the Good News that We are Rescued from God's Wrath through Jesus Christ the Lord! There is only one, true way to be rescued through Jesus Christ, it is by accepting Him as Lord. Romans 14:9 reveals, "To this end Christ died and rose and lived again, that He might be Lord of both the dead and the living."

Jesus went to the cross, not merely to offer us forgiveness and a place in heaven, but to reclaim His position as Lord. This is the essential conflict of sin: it dethrones the Son of God from His Lordship over our lives. By removing our guilt, however, God restores our relationship and reestablishes His authority. He becomes Lord of our lives. Those who only regard Jesus as a Savior, but refuse His authority as Lord, have not truly been converted. They have not truly been saved.

This is why faith and repentance are inextricably intertwined.

Act 3:19 tells us: "Repent therefore and be converted, that your sins may be blotted out." True faith is demonstrated by the actions it produces. James 2:17 says, "Faith without works is dead." Mere intellectual agreement, with a few points of theology, is not enough to save, there must be "conversion." James 2:19 goes on to say, "The demons believe—and tremble!" Satan knows Jesus died and rose from the dead—but he's not saved. Repentance is proof that one's faith is credible. Repentance demonstrates that a man has turned away from his sin, renounced lifestyle choices that offend God, and submitted his will to the Lordship of Jesus Christ. Repentance demonstrates that one's faith has converted him from a life of sinful rebellion to a life of submission to Christ.

This is the gospel: it's the good news that we are rescued from God's wrath through Jesus Christ the Lord.

A DIFFERENT GOSPEL

The true gospel will stand for eternity. Scripture tells us that heaven and earth may pass away, but the Word of the Lord endures forever (Matthew 24:35). Our concern, however, is not with the truth, it's with those who present it. Today, more than ever, we are seeing a reluctance to speak truth to our culture with clarity and persuasion. Instead, leaders have acquired a skillful ambiguity that avoids controversy and deflects difficult conversations. They call it "tolerance" and "compassion." Maybe it is. Or, maybe it's cowardice and a failure to lead. Maybe it's how the gospel becomes perverted.

When Paul admonished that "savage wolves" would come and "a different gospel" would rise, he was alerting the church to forces that would pervert the truth by penetrating the church's culture. More specifically, he was speaking to "elders" and admonishing them to confront error when it comes. Unfortunately, history reveals that many leaders failed to confront error and the gospel, as well as the church, was overrun by the corrupt systems of the world. It wasn't until the 16th century when reformers would call the church back to the ideals of "Sola Scriptura."[2]

Therefore, as we identify the cultural pressure points of today, and the 21st-century savage wolves hounding for entry, we must recognize our vulnerability. The places where we have departed from sound doctrine and orthodoxy will become the gateways through which delusion gains a foothold. The elders and leaders who offer no response to the deception at our door will be the ones inviting the wolves to dine at our table.

Today, there are four areas of fallacy that need to be addressed in the modern gospel—four errors that are providing fertile soil for deception to rise in the church: an over-emphasis on man, an extreme view of grace, an avoidance of offense, and an apathy toward repentance.

An Over-Emphasis on Man

It has been called the "Anthropocentric Gospel." "Anthropos" is the Greek word for "man," specifically "mankind" as a group. The word "centric" means "centered upon." Simply put, "anthropocentric" means "centered on mankind." In an Anthropocentric Gospel, the value of the message is determined by how it improves or benefits humans. It exegetes scripture from man's perspective, designs worship to emphasize man's experience, offers prayers for man's benefit, predicts a future for man's fulfillment, and interprets life events from man's vantage point. It's all about man—mans' happiness, mans' desires, mans' destiny, mans' glory. The glory of God, the will and purpose of God, are mere byproducts of mans' complete satisfaction.

The counterapproach is "theocentrism." "Theo" means "God." In this perspective, meaning and value are derived from God being at the center. All experiences are interpreted through His word, from His purposes, and for His glory. Theocentrism begins with God and has human experience at the periphery. Preaching provokes sanctification. Worship magnifies God. Church is a place to serve. Tithing is a privilege. Generosity is a discipline. One's talents are offered in service to the King and never, never does man receive the praise.

Take a cursory view of the church landscape today and you will find a strong anthropocentric gospel. Rather than centering on the sovereignty, majesty, and authority of God, many churches present God as mostly concerned about man's happiness and success. The power and wisdom of God are turned upon man for his benefit and personal achievement. It's the gospel of being number one, overcoming obstacles, finding your joy, discovering your purpose, and achieving your greatness. One famous preacher described his destiny as "helping you reach your destiny." This is anthropocentrism at its best. The preacher believes he exists to help every man achieve his own personal aspirations—whatever they may be.

More interesting is what the preacher did not say. He did not say his purpose was to help you achieve Christlikeness or to walk fully in the will of God or become effective in bringing souls to Christ. No—in the anthropocentric gospel, those issues are tangential. The man-centered gospel implies that the reason for everything is the happiness of man—your happiness. It's a gospel of humanism. God should make you happy. Church should meet your needs. Programs should serve your interests. Worship should inspire you. Preaching should encourage you. People should love you. Just take a look at some of the most popular recommended sermon titles on a church marketing website: "Praying Will Bring You Peace, Forgiveness Frees You From Bitterness, Sex God's Way is Safe, Satisfying and Sizzling, God Will Bring Good Out of Your Suffering, God Has a Hope and Future for You."[3] The common theme is man-centered and the benefits man receives.

From a marketing perspective, it's a savvy strategy. From a biblical perspective, it's idolatry. It breeds the notion that God exists for my needs and happiness. It undermines the ethic to serve and sacrifice for the benefit of community. It promotes the belief that community should serve me, and others exist for my needs. It was an attitude that Jesus confronted directly when he said, "Most assuredly, I say to you, you seek Me, not because you saw the signs, but because you ate of the loaves and were filled" (John 6:26). In other words, "You're not following Me because I'm the Son of God, you're following Me because of what I can do for you." It's an ideology that provides fertile soil for a self-styled gospel that caters to each person's lifestyle choices, moral preferences, and personal desires. It's not the gospel; it's idolatry.

An Extreme View of Grace

It's called the "Hyper-Grace Movement." It's a movement in modern Christianity that places an extreme emphasis on the grace of God in the believer's life. Hyper-grace teaches that sin is a non-issue for believers because the atonement provides forgiveness for one's future sins in the same way it forgives one's past sins. Some proponents even teach that confessing and repenting from sin are unnecessary because Christians are in a perpetual state of forgiveness. Sin, they say, is only offensive to God because it may be unhealthy for a believer—it's more of a disappointment to God because the sinning Christian is impairing himself. Even more, the doctrine of sanctification, which teaches that believers are progressively set apart from the world by the Holy Spirit and conformed to the image of Christ, is dismissed by hyper-grace teachers as legalism.

In reality, sin is an issue for the believer, not because it disappoints God, but because it offends Him, grieves Him and hinders our fellowship with Him. Grace does not blind God to the reality of our sin. Although it's true that "where sin abounds, grace abounds much more," (Romans 5:20); it is also true that sin in the believer's life is toxic and deadly, regardless of how much grace is present. For example, disunity in marriage hinders prayer. Unbelief hardens the heart. Unforgiveness interferes with worship. Hatred of a brother holds one in darkness. Unequal yokes drag us down. Sexual immorality defiles our body, and fellowship with evil people corrupts good morals. Clearly, the grace of God doesn't discount personal responsibility and consequences for sin.

Practical matters like obedience and holiness are realities for the disciple of Christ. We are called to "Walk worthy of the Lord, fully pleasing Him, being fruitful in every good work and increasing in the knowledge of God" (Colossians 1:10). We are commanded to "Put to death your members which are on the earth: fornication, uncleanness, passion, evil desire, and covetousness, which is idolatry" (Colossians 3:5). We are exhorted to "Put on the whole armor of God, that you may be able to stand against the wiles of the devil (Ephesians 6:11). Peter reminds us to "Be sober, be vigilant; because your adversary the devil walks about like a roaring lion, seeking whom he may devour. Resist him, steadfast in the faith" (1 Peter 5:8-9).

This is not a new issue for the church. The Apostle Paul dealt with a form of hyper-grace known as antinomianism in Romans 6. The word antinomianism comes from two Greek words, anti, meaning "against"; and nomos, meaning "law." Antinomianism means "against the law." It is the belief that there are no moral laws God expects Christians to obey. This is unbiblical. God expects us to live a life of righteousness, integrity, and love. His grace does free us from the commands of Mosaic Law, but does not provide a license to sin. On the contrary, it empowers us to overcome sin and cultivate righteousness, depending on the Holy Spirit to help us. 1 John 2:3-6 declares, "Now by this we know that we know Him, if we keep His commandments. He who says, "I know Him," and does not keep His commandments, is a liar, and the truth is not in him. But whoever keeps His word, truly the love of God is perfected in him. By this we know that we are in Him. He who says he abides in Him ought himself also to walk just as He walked." Salvation comes by grace, but obedience and personal responsibility are factors in our perseverance and sanctification.

Such an extreme view of grace opens the door to subtle deception. Dogmatic views of doctrinal purity are viewed as legalistic or narrow-minded as the greater focus is placed on themes such as love, mercy, and tolerance. These themes are crucial, but when untempered by discernment and orthodoxy, they become gateways for any worldly philosophy to gain a foothold because "accepting people" becomes more important than discerning the ideals those people bring.

An Avoidance of Offense

Tolerance is a good thing. It means you put up with and bear with, people of different views and values, or people who live lifestyles you believe to be wrong. If you are a Christian, tolerance means you will be kind toward those with whom you disagree. You will bear with them, respect them and treat them with honor, despite the fact you oppose the values they represent.

Tolerance is how a society maintains peace and order. It's how people of different races, cultures, and beliefs can exist together without tearing each other apart. You respect them, and you speak well of them, even though you disagree with their lifestyle choices. In fact, tolerance is commanded in scripture. Ephesians 4:2-3 says "With all lowliness and gentleness, with longsuffering, [bear] with one another in love, endeavoring to keep the unity of the Spirit in the bond of peace." Words such as "longsuffering," "bearing with," and "endeavoring to keep" suggest there is some disagreement, or contention, or even offense. But these feelings are overcome in order to achieve unity overall.

Unfortunately, tolerance has been redefined in today's social-justice-warrior-culture. The new tolerance is not merely putting up with different views and lifestyles, but accepting and agreeing with those lifestyles, and regarding them as just as true as our own. Even more, if you don't accept those beliefs as valid and true, you are branded as a hater, a bigot, a homophobe, a racist, and a xenophobe. The world will mock your faith and ask accusingly, "What kind of 'Christian' are you? Aren't you supposed to love and accept everyone? How can you call yourself 'religious' and judge others?"

But loving someone does not mean you must accept and agree with that person's lifestyle. Such a notion is absolute nonsense. It is possible to disagree with someone without hating them. It is possible to love someone while opposing their choices and beliefs. Parents do this all the time—as do friends. You can believe someone is totally wrong and disagree with them while at the same time caring about them, respecting them and honoring them as a special creation of God.

Unfortunately, many in the church have accepted the lie that to love someone means you can never offend them. This is especially true of many pastors. Sermons are carefully scripted to avoid any issues that may stir controversy or make people feel badly about their lifestyles. Messages are designed to validate and affirm—to tell people how much God loves them and wants them to be happy. There is no definition of right and wrong. There is no mention of sin, rebellious living, the wrath of God or coming judgment—not in sermons, not in books, not on talk shows, not on social media—there is nothing that would offend or make anyone feel bad about themselves. In fact, any attempt to address practical issues of obedience is condemned as moralism and is becoming taboo in church culture.

The problem is, not only does this misrepresent the gospel and the nature of God, it removes the cutting edge of the gospel—that which gives it the power to produce repentance. Sadly, without repentance, there is no conversion and without conversion, there is no salvation. Without salvation, all we have is a crowd of unconverted sinners believing God accepts them just the way they are, with no intention to make Jesus Christ Lord of their lives.

An Apathy toward Repentance

The gospel is not a "good idea." The gospel is not good therapy. It is not a convenient option. The gospel is good news—it's the news that we are under the wrath and judgment of God, but Jesus Christ rescued us through the cross.

When this news is heard and understood, there is only one appropriate response: repentance. Faced with the knowledge that sin put us under the penalty of eternal damnation, knowing that sin is what sent Jesus to the cross, learning that sin is what destroyed creation and placed us under a curse, should produce the result of remorse, regret, and determination to never live as a slave to sin again.

This is repentance. The Greek word is "metanoia." It means a "change of heart." It is a directional term that implies one is altering their course; they are taking a new direction. From it's very beginning, the gospel and repentance are inseparable. Jesus was the first to connect the two in Mark 1:5 when He said, "The time is fulfilled, and the kingdom of God is at hand. Repent, and believe in the gospel." Peter commanded repentance in Acts 3:19: "Repent therefore and be converted, that your sins may be blotted out, so that times of refreshing may come from the presence of the Lord." Paul traveled "Throughout all the region of Judea, and then to the Gentiles, [preaching] that they should repent, turn to God, and do works befitting repentance" (Acts 26:20).

Unfortunately, the gospel today rarely mentions it. It's not because preachers don't believe in repentance, it's because what they preach does not produce it. Most preaching today is about how God will help you, bless you, fill you, love you, and make you succeed. The gospel today is centered on man's comfort and the benefits one receives by allowing God into one's life. Jesus is a utility, like a good mechanic or a plumber. He will help your family, fix your finances, boost your career and make you a much happier, more fulfilled person.

Sadly, that's not the gospel. That's self-help theory. That's life-coaching. That's a sales pitch. God is indeed good and blesses those who trust in Him, but that is secondary. The primary truth of the gospel is this: we have broken the laws of God and are guilty. God is holy and must punish our sins. But God in His love provided rescue through His Son. This is where the gospel begins—not with how much God can bless us or how much He can help us—it begins with the law. It begins with the fact that we are guilty, under God's judgment and desperately needing salvation.

An accurate presentation of the gospel must begin with an accurate understanding of God's law. It presents the legal and religious standard that God gives us and shows us that we can never fulfill it. The law shows us our depravity and need for a savior. Paul wrote, "The law was our tutor to bring us to Christ, that we might be justified by faith" (Galatians 3:24). He also wrote, "I would not have known sin except through the law" (Romans 7:7). Unfortunately, most "gospel messages" today do not even mention the law of God or mankind's guilt. Therefore, man has no knowledge of his lost condition, his peril under the wrath of God, and his need to repent. To most people hearing the gospel today, God is an eager friend, a generous uncle, or a tail wagging puppy who only wants us to feel warm and cozy.

WHICH JESUS? WHICH GOSPEL?

"Multitudes came to Christ! Dozens accepted Jesus!" It's a common post by pastors on social media that always leaves me wondering, "What 'Jesus' did they accept?" If the Apostle Paul questioned those at Corinth who preached "another Jesus" from a "different gospel," then I think we can do the same.

Which Jesus did they accept? Did they accept the healing Jesus who removes your pain? Did they accept the caring Jesus who gives you a better life? Did they accept the providing Jesus who gets you a job? Did they accept the guiding Jesus who solves your problems or the loving Jesus who takes everyone to heaven, no conditions attached? Which Jesus did they accept? Pastor Kenneth Neal said it best:

> There is another Jesus that the world loves to follow. He allows everyone into heaven, he doesn't require obedience, he doesn't require holiness, he doesn't require repentance, he never says anything offensive, he calls everyone his children, he will not send anyone to hell, he wants you to do your own will, he does not have any commandments only suggestions, you don't have to pay tithes, you can keep all your money and spend it on yourself, and you don't even have to go to church to live for him, if you are following this Jesus, I just thought I would let you know that his real name is… Satan!

Unfortunately, the "Jesus" commonly preached today is a figment of motivational talks and self-help theories presented by pastors as life-coaches dispensing advice on how to succeed and achieve your dreams. Lost souls, sin-sick from the toxic lies of the world, come to our churches for gospel truth and we offer them advice for a happy marriage and better career. They're starving for spiritual food and we say, "Do these five things and you'll feel better" or, "Here are seven steps to success." Sure, it's covered over with evangelical terms and smattered about with scriptures, but it lacks the quickening, cutting, piercing power that a sharp two-edged sword should have. We are churning out pseudo-converts who agreed intellectually with a few points of theology—something about a virgin birth and another something about an empty grave—but they cannot endure sound doctrine, they cannot tolerate repentance, they cannot handle the call to the cross because we've acclimated them to a soothing gospel that itches their ears. We feel good because we think we're offering something practical and pragmatic, but it's not preparing them for eternity, much less for cultural warfare. Leonard Ravenhill said it best: "Tragically, hell will be filled with people who've learned, from modern-day preachers, how to be happy and achieve success."

"Well, we don't want to offend or drive people away; we want to reach them." But there can be no salvation without repentance; there can be no repentance without conviction; and there can be no conviction without a preacher preaching the inspired, anointed, uncompromised, full counsel of the Word of God. Romans 10:14 says, "How then shall they call on Him if they've not believed? And how shall they believe if they've not heard? And how shall they hear without a preacher?"

Just to be perfectly clear, here's the gospel. We are sinners, guilty and lost, on our way to an eternal Hell under the wrath of God. There is only one name under heaven, given among men by which we must be saved. It's not the name of Buddha, Mohammad, Shiva, or any other. Jesus is the name. Jesus went to the cross, bore our sins, suffered the wrath of God meant for us, died the death we deserved, and rose on the third day to demonstrate the power of His atoning blood. He ascended to the Father and now offers eternal life.

It's not about fulfilling your dreams or giving you your best life now; it's not about help for your problems or advice for your career, it's about being lost and needing to be found. It's about being dead in sin and needing a new life. It's about a Savior who paid your debt and placing your trust in what He did on the cross. It's about receiving by faith, not only what He did, but who He is: The Lord, almighty God, who sits on the throne of our lives.

Pressure Points

two
MORALITY AND TRUTH

There's no one way to be a man. Men who get their periods are men. Men who get pregnant and give birth are men. Trans and non-binary men belong. #InternationalMensDay
- ACLU Tweet

Beware lest anyone cheat you through philosophy and empty deceit, according to the tradition of men, according to the basic principles of the world, and not according to Christ.
- Colossians 2:8

"Sexual relations between two men is wrong!" "Abortion is immoral!" "Sex outside of marriage is sin." These are extremely controversial and polarizing statements regarding hot-topic issues in today's world. Dare to make such sweeping declarations and you better be prepared for intense verbal combat.

The reason why people defend these issues so fiercely is not necessarily because they are practicing homosexuality or planning to have an abortion, the reason is "Moral Relativism." Moral relativism is a belief system that rejects the idea of moral absolutes or objective principles of right and wrong. It teaches that each person must determine "their own truth" and achieve their own morality based on personal preference and subjective experience. Those who advocate this philosophy will often say, "To each his own," "Who are you to judge?" or, "Don't impose your morals on me."

Moral Relativism is a major tenet of modern culture. We live in a time when no one has the right to call anyone else's beliefs or behaviors wrong. If you do, you are "judging," or are accused of having some kind of cultural phobia. As a result, western society has introduced a new form of enlightenment called "being woke."

It means one has been awakened to an awareness of certain social issues that are on the proper side of political correctness. Originally, "staying woke" meant you were aware of racial injustice, in current culture however, the application has broadened. Today, being "woke," means you champion a woman's right to abort her unborn child, or you celebrate trans-children who want to surgically alter their gender, or you advocate for redefining marriage and family in a way that advances the homosexual agenda. And if you dare to disagree—if you would be so bold as to say that such things are "wrong"—those in the woke culture will brand you as a bigot, racist, fascist, misogynist, homophobic, transphobic, conservatard fundie (a fundie is a pejorative for a religious fundamentalist, especially a Christian fundamentalist). Fail to acknowledge a woman's "right to choose" or a teenager's right to change their gender and you will be marginalized and ostracized as an ignoramus who has forfeited his or her right to express an opinion.

Every day it seems that pop culture has discovered a new woke value that contradicts logic and anyone who insists on logic is shamed, insulted and punished into submission. Indeed, we have entered the age of two plus two equals five. In 1949, George Orwell wrote a classic depiction of dystopian future called *1984*.[1] In it, the main character, Winston Smith is being "re-educated" by society's controlling authority known as "Big Brother." His educator holds up four fingers and asks him how many he sees. Smith responds with the correct number but is punished with an electric shock. Through the pain, he asks, "How can I see anything but four? Two plus two equals four." To which, his educator responds, "Yes, sometimes two plus two is four. But sometimes it's five or even three. Sometimes it's all of those at the same time." Distraught by this confusion, Winston is told that all reality is relative. More specifically, reality is defined by the powers that control society. If society wants two plus two to equal four, then it will be four. If it's five, then it's five. As the scene plays out, Smith is shocked continually until he surrenders and admits to seeing five fingers, not four. But the punishment persists. "You are only telling me what you think I want to hear," his teacher insists. "You have to really believe there are five."

Moral relativism is shocking us daily with what is completely absurd and illogical. To the one whose only agenda is truth, the tenets of homosexuality, transgenderism, and abortion just don't add up. Two plus two equals four, not five. But in a culture where morality is relative and people have an agenda to push their own personal truth, the math can add up to anything they want it to. In *1984*, it was called the *Ministry of Truth* or *Propaganda*. Today it's the media, politics and pop culture. After you've heard the insanity of moral relativism over and over—and after you've been made to suffer for not agreeing with it—you will eventually submit and accept the absurd notions of a deluded culture. The ACLU recently tweeted that men can have a menstrual cycle.[2] Planned Parenthood insists that what a pregnant woman has in her womb is not actual, human life. The LGBTQ community would have us agree that homosexuality is natural—that God created people that way. It's nonsense. But the fact that these issues do not make sense doesn't matter. All that matters is we join with woke culture and make ourselves actually believe that two plus two equals five.

A HISTORY OF MORAL RELATIVISM

From a biblical perspective, moral relativism is nothing new. As far back as the Book of Judges, mankind has asserted its right to determine morality apart from an absolute or divine standard. The concluding verse, Judges 21:25, sums it up: "In those days there was no king in Israel; everyone did what was right in his own eyes." It was a time when God's people choose their own morality over the Word of God and suffered severe oppression and national conflict because of it.

Even after Mosaic Law codified principles of morality, there were people who refused to accept it. Around 700 BC, the prophet Isaiah lamented those who corrupted the nation by their moral indifference. He cried, "Woe to those who call evil good, and good evil; who put darkness for light, and light for darkness; who put bitter for sweet, and sweet for bitter! Woe to those who are wise in their own eyes, and prudent in their own sight!" (Isaiah 5:20-21).

The philosophy of moral relativism was not unique to ancient

Israel, it developed into a philosophy in fifth-century Greece. The historian, Herodotus, records an anecdote in which Darius, King of Persia, gathered the Greeks in his court and asked them if they could be convinced to eat the dead bodies of their fathers. Appalled, they said they could never do that—not for any amount of money. Later, Darius asked some Indians from the tribe of Callatiae, who regularly ate the bodies of their dead parents, if they would consider burning those bodies instead. They uttered a cry of disgust and forbade him to mention such a dreadful thing. Herodotus drew the conclusion that morality must be relative. Some behavior may be right for some and wrong for others based upon their culture and orientation.[3]

According to Herodotus, right and wrong are defined solely by culture and personal preference. The Greeks (as well as those from the Book of Judges and Isaiah's day) would have us believe that morality is an individual choice that varies from one society to another. They would say there are no universal standards, no absolute rules, everyone is free to do what is right in their own sight, as dictated by their culture and conscience. This is the essence of moral relativism, two plus two can equal whatever we want it to.

It is certainly true that some morals are unique to the culture from which they come. In that sense, morality is relative when it expresses locally developed styles and preferences of individuals, groups, or societies. But where do we draw the line on such morality? What about Nazi Germany? Did not Hitler's culture teach that the "Final Solution" of exterminating millions of Jews was moral in their society? And then there's Al Qaeda and the Taliban who supported them. Their culture believed it was moral to fly planes into buildings, killing over 3,000 people, on September 11, 2001. If morality is relative, how can we judge the Nazis or Al Qaeda, or even the Hutu Tribe of Rwanda, who slaughtered one million of their Tutsi neighbors, because of the cultural differences?

The logic doesn't stand because there is one all-important element missing from worldly philosophy: the authority of God. There is a God who exists as the Sovereign Power over the universe and commands mankind's obedience to His laws. This is where we "draw the line" between right and wrong—not culture, not each person's conscience—but the Word of God. The Bible is the defining rule for mankind's morality and provides absolutes that transcend culture or personal preference. These are the truths that give Christ's followers a firm sense of conviction in a culture that has lost its moral compass.

But remove God from the equation and man assumes he is free to do anything he wants and live any way he desires. The result? Chaos ensues—the depravity of man hijacks the culture and brings oppression, genocide, and tyranny. This is exactly what moral relativism does. It rejects the authority of a Creator and releases men from accountability to His laws. It deletes God entirely from the equation and places man as his own sovereign rule. And man, left to himself, is not a benevolent ruler.

Despite this, from the days of the ancient Hebrew Judges to modern-day western culture, moral relativism has great appeal. In the book, *The Day America Told the Truth,* James Patterson asked a random group of Americans the question: "What are you willing to do for 10 million dollars?" The results were quite revealing. 25 percent would abandon their family, 23 percent would become prostitutes for a week, 16 percent would give up their American citizenships, 16 percent would leave their spouses, 10 percent would withhold testimony to let a murderer go free, 7 percent would kill a stranger and 3 percent would put their children up for adoption.[4] Additional research from the University of Utah, together with Harvard researchers found that individuals who could gain monetarily through unethical behavior were more likely to demonstrate that behavior and justify it based on their financial gain.[5]

One might say, "But wait, prostitution is wrong, divorce is wrong, murder is wrong, financial maleficence is wrong." Apparently, these are wrong only if you believe in moral absolutes. A large percentage of the population is not interested in what is right as a universal principle, they are only interested in what is "right for them, in a particular moment." In other words, right and wrong are not decided objectively, right and wrong are decided by what best serves each person's interests at that time. Morality is relative and subjective. "If being honest helps me advance my career, I'll be honest. If not, I'll lie." Or, "If being pregnant suits my lifestyle, I'll keep the baby. If it's inconvenient, I'll abort it. Or, "If being married makes me happy, I'll stay with my wife. If not, I'll leave her and find someone who fulfills me."

Moral relativism is popular today simply because so many people want the freedom to define right and wrong based on their own desires. We don't want a God telling us how to live our lives and holding us accountable for the choices we've made.

MORAL RELATIVISM VERSES RELATIVE MORALISM

It is important to note that addressing moral relativism in the culture should not become an exercise in moralism. Moralism is an extreme emphasis on morality that attempts to impose one's own morals on others. In the church, moralizing occurs when moral conformity is emphasized to such extremes that obedience precedes faith and grace is obscured. It looks a lot like legalism which stresses religious performance and adherence to laws and traditions. Moralism is a form of heresy that elevates one's moral conduct as more essential to his or her salvation than faith in the atoning work of Christ. In fact, avoidance of moralism is one reason why some pastors sidestep addressing immorality in both church and culture entirely. To them, remaining silent on morality is theological high ground and a better portrayal of the gospel.

To be clear, the gospel is not moralism. Keeping commands and following rules are not what brings cleansing from sin. Romans 3:20 clearly states, "By the deeds of the law no flesh will be justified in His sight." The ineffectiveness of morality to cleanse a sinner is clear—it cannot. Only the blood of Jesus Christ can do that. The believer's security is based upon the work of Christ, not his or her ability to live moral lives—this is the central message of the gospel.

Furthermore, it is not the church's role to police the morals of society. We live in a fallen world, and we can never hope to imbue society with our sense of morality, be it personal or biblical. Our primary calling is to preach the gospel, which awakens the lost to their moral bankruptcy and provokes repentance.

This is not to say that those who preach the gospel can never address issues of morality. Obviously, there are circumstances when leaders must denounce certain evils in the world, especially when those evils are imprinting in the church, putrefying culture, and perpetuating suffering on others. Such is the purpose of this book. In fact, there are four important reasons why church leaders today need to tackle these difficult topics in a practical and relevant way.

First, sanctification informs the morality of the believer. Clearly, good morals and religious works do not save one's soul. Salvation is solely through the blood of Jesus Christ applied to the believer by faith. But the purpose of salvation is not simply to forgive sins and get souls into heaven, the purpose of salvation is to bring people into a relationship with God, through the Holy Spirit, and conform them to the image of Christ. Indeed, this will affect one's sense of morality. Ephesians 2:8-10 says, "For by grace you have been saved through faith, and that not of yourselves; it is the gift of God, not of works, lest anyone should boast. For we are His workmanship, created in Christ Jesus for good works, which God prepared beforehand that we should walk in them." Essentially, we are not saved "by" our good works, we are saved "for" good works. As we are made alive in Christ, we are set apart as His servants to be sanctified by His word, through His Spirit, for His glory. Pastors, preachers, church leaders have a responsibility to teach the morals of God's Word so believers "May walk worthy of the Lord, fully pleasing Him, being fruitful in every good work" (Colossians 1:10).

Second, leaders must inform the cultural morality in the church. In each of Paul's epistles to the churches, along with those of James, Peter, John and the author of Hebrews, these leaders are attempting to establish appropriate norms and taboos for church culture. Paul instructed the Corinthians to "Not to keep company with anyone named a brother, who is sexually immoral, or covetous, or an idolater, or a reviler, or a drunkard, or an extortioner—not even to eat with such a person" (1 Corinthians 5:11). Peter was concerned about false teachers in the world and he told believers to be "persons of holiness and godliness" (2 Peter 3:11). James was aware of the influence the world was having on the church and wrote: "Adulterers and adulteresses! Do you not know that friendship with the world is enmity with God? Whoever therefore wants to be a friend of the world makes himself an enemy of God" (James 4:4). As well, John reminded his readers: "Do not love the world or the things in the world. If anyone loves the world, the love of the Father is not in him. For all that is in the world—the lust of the flesh, the lust of the eyes, and the pride of life—is not of the Father but is of the world" (1 John 2:15-16).

These leaders recognized it was their duty to shape church culture by emphasizing the behaviors that are desired—and it's no different today. Every church needs a leader whose example sets the tone for the congregation to follow. His or her values, and the messages spoken, are what establishes norms and taboos. This is especially true regarding cultural pressure points in the church. Leaders who speak directly to issues will intentionally shape culture. Those who do not, put their church—and the disciples they are called to train—at risk.

Third, as salt and light, the church informs the morality of culture. Jesus said, "You are the salt of the earth; but if the salt loses its flavor, how shall it be seasoned? It is then good for nothing but to be thrown out and trampled underfoot by men. You are the light of the world. A city that is set on a hill cannot be hidden. Nor do they light a lamp and put it under a basket, but on a lampstand, and it gives light to all who are in the house. Let your light so shine before men, that they may see your good works and glorify your Father in heaven" (Matthew 5:13-16). Clearly, Jesus expected His church to be an influence in culture. Salt is a preservative that prevents decay in meat that would otherwise rot, and light is an element that dispels darkness wherever it is present. By describing His followers as salt and light, Jesus was explaining our role in society as a restraining force in the world, standing in the gap, attempting to prevent the incipient nature of sin from metastasizing mankind. Pastors who refuse to speak directly to moral issues are abdicating their role as a leader and are surrendering their influence on the culture of the world. We need only to recall the influence of the church throughout history on matters of slavery, genocide and civil rights to understand its importance in the world.

Fourth, emphasizing morality informs mankind of its sin and need for a Savior. When the church addresses issues of morality, it is not an attempt to "moralize" culture or, for that matter, people. We recognize that lost people are just that—lost. They are dead in sin and separated from God (Ephesians 2:5). Attempting to improve them by improving their morals is no different than trying to improve a corpse by dressing it in new clothes. No matter how good it looks on the outside, it is still dead. This is man's condition apart from salvation and no amount of good works or high morals can improve that. Only repentance and new life in Christ can bring spiritual rebirth.

Addressing issues of morality does, however, have a role in the process of prevenient grace and salvation. The Apostle Paul, said, "The law was our tutor to bring us to Christ, that we might be justified by faith" (Galatians 3:24). He goes on to say, "By the law is the knowledge of sin" (Romans 3:20). When a lost sinner is confronted with the truth that his behavior is immoral—that he violates the law of God—it provides the opportunity for the Holy Spirit to "convict [him] of sin, and of righteousness, and of judgment" (John 16:8). This is how true conversion takes place. The lost soul realizes its guilt before a holy God, feels the burden of judgment to come, repents from a life of sin, and surrenders to the Lordship of Jesus Christ.

Sadly, many presentations of the gospel neglect this all-important truth. Rather than calling out issues of sin or speaking of judgment to come, some preachers hope to win people through a more palatable presentation. The "gospel" is presented as a happy pill for one's discouragement or unhappiness; God is described as a helpful friend that brings success to your career, restores love to your marriage, offers you purpose and fulfillment, achieves your destiny, or generally helps you live your best life now. While there is some truth to these "offers" and they may attract people to church for a season, this "gospel" does not convince lost souls of guilt, it does not produce repentance from sin, it does not result in submission to Christ as Lord, and it does not generate a sanctified life bearing the fruit of the Spirit. This is why so many churches today are populated with unconverted members who enjoy the motivational messages, love the lights and music, and are encouraged by the fellowship; but sadly, have no relationship with God. They may have been baptized, they may have become members, but they have never heard the true good news, which is the remedy for the bad news, and their need to repent, submit to Christ, be transformed by His Word, and sealed in His Spirit.

MORAL RELATIVISM IN THE CHURCH

It should come as no surprise that the secular world has embraced a naturalistic worldview steeped in moral relativism. We should expect that from a culture broken by sin and separated from God since the fall of man. What is alarming, however, is how moral relativism is creeping into the church.

More and more, we are seeing believers becoming less dogmatic about Bible truth and more tolerant of worldliness. Attitudes toward divorce and remarriage, homosexuality, cohabitation, and other moral issues are becoming acceptable. While it is good that Christians are loving and tolerant toward those who struggle with these issues, it is not good that we are redefining what the Bible calls "sin" as "choices each person must make for himself or herself." This is my greatest concern: it's not the secular world's rejection of absolute truth, it is the church's ignorance of biblical truth.

A recent article for FoxNews.com asked, "Why are so many Christians biblically illiterate?"[6] The article exposed a growing trend among American churchgoers: they are not reading the Bible; and therefore, they don't know what it says. A report from LifeWay Research revealed only 45 percent of those who regularly attend church read the Bible more than once a week, over 40 percent of the people attending church read their Bible occasionally, maybe once or twice a month, and almost 1 in 5 churchgoers say they never read the Bible.[7]

While it's expected that unsaved people have little or no Bible knowledge, it's alarming that the church is equally ignorant. Life-

Way Research found that while evangelicals believe heaven is a real place, 20 percent believe Jesus Christ is not the only way to get there. As well, more than half of evangelicals (59 percent) believe the Holy Spirit is a force and not a divine, personal being—in contrast to the biblical doctrine of the Trinity which teaches three Persons in one God.[8] Add to this a Barna Research Group report in which almost half of Millennials (47 percent) believe it is wrong to evangelize,[9] and another Barna survey in which many Christians can name only two or three of the disciples and fewer than half of all adults can name the four gospels. Still another study shows 60 percent cannot name five of the Ten Commandments. George Barna states, "No wonder people break the Ten Commandments all the time. They don't know what they are."[10]

THE PERIL OF BIBLICAL ILLITERACY

It is clear to see how moral relativism is sweeping through the church: Christians are not learning the Bible. And if we don't know what truth is, how can we follow it—let alone stand for it in society? This is why so many churches—and believers—compromise on issues of homosexuality, divorce and remarriage, cohabitation, and even abortion. Not learning scripture results in not knowing it which gives moral relativism a clear path into the church.

Something needs to change—and churches must take responsibility. While true that Bible learning must begin at home, studies show that Christians who lack Bible knowledge are products of churches that marginalize Bible teaching. In an attempt to be "attractional" and retain visitors, many church services today focus more on music, media, and entertainment, while less time is given to teaching the Word of God. Small group ministry can help remedy this, but unfortunately, many of these groups never get beyond superficial topics. Even worship music today is largely devoid of scripture. Many contemporary lyrics convey themes that cater to emotions and have little impact on the worshipper's ability to learn and retain God's Word. One very popular "worship song" even promotes the Theory of Evolution. The net result is a community of believers that is biblically confused, spiritually malnourished, ignorant of the truth, and unable to discern the lies of the enemy—even while living in the midst of them.

Tragically, the group most victimized by the decline in Bible teaching is the church's younger generation. In an attempt to keep youth engaged, many youth ministries focus on games, entertainment, and social interaction. Bible teaching is relegated to a few minutes that has little or no impact on teenagers' spiritual development. The themes are often designed to amuse by mimicking pop culture and rarely deal with serious issues. The result is an adult generation of Millennials and Gen Zs that think doctrine is antiquated, evangelism is offensive, and church attendance unnecessary.

Sadly, many youth leaders are catering to this trend by pretending that teenagers are unable to learn deeper truths, and are, therefore, unwilling to challenge them. But not only are young people capable of learning deeper truths; it is exactly what they need. If youth can learn algebra, history and English comp, they can learn doctrine, theology and the deeper truths of God's Word. Teach them scripture! Make it relevant, keep it interesting, use skillful teachers—but by all means, equip young people with truth and morality. If we fail to do so, the next generation of churchgoers will be lost to the pressures of moral relativism.

While the church does bear responsibility, parents must be reminded that the duty to disciple their children lies squarely on them. It is not the pastor's job to disciple your kids. It's your job. The church will support you, help you, and reinforce what you teach, but parents must be the primary trainers in their child's spiritual education. Deuteronomy 6:7 says, "You shall teach [God's commands] diligently to your children, and shall talk of them when you sit in your house, when you walk by the way, when you lie down, and when you rise up." Proverbs 22:6 tells us, "Train up a child in the way he should go, and when he is old he will not depart from it." Paul wrote, "And you, fathers [and mothers], do not provoke your children to wrath, but bring them up in the training and admonition of the Lord" (Ephesians 6:4). Parents, as good as your church may be, you cannot delegate this responsibility to the children's ministry or the youth pastor. God assigned this duty to you—and it is non-negotiable. Children must see their parents as teachers and fellow students of God's Word.

Congregations and parishioners also assume responsibility for a church that champions the Bible. Learn how to encourage pastors and teachers who faithfully expound the scriptures. Become active listeners and stay engaged. Learn how to say "Amen" and tell your preacher to "Preach it!" Most people never realize the struggle that pastors have when preparing and presenting the word. Congregations who sit motionless, distracted, disinterested and disengaged only convince their preachers that their preaching is barely tolerable. Sit up, lean in, take notes, feed on the Word. And when the preaching is good, be sure to tell your pastor how good it is. Give him or her positive feedback. Remember that the devil is always tormenting your pastor with his lies: "That sermon was dull. The content was boring. Those examples were offensive. The people think you're long-winded." Be an armor-bearer, be a warrior, counter the devil's tactics to weaken the pulpit of your church. Encourage the preacher: send a card, write an email, text a message, put a post on Facebook or a picture on Instagram. Let your pastor know how much you appreciate a strong, anointed, well-prepared, well-delivered message from the Word of God.

RECLAIMING OUR CHRISTIAN WORLDVIEW

Abortion. Euthanasia. Same-sex marriage. Transgenderism. Cohabitation: how you view these issues is largely determined by your "worldview." A worldview is how you view the world, not in the physical sense, but in the philosophical sense. It's a set of basic assumptions we make about the world around us and we interpret the world through those assumptions.

There are two predominant worldviews in western society: naturalism and theism (although theism is rapidly diminishing). Theism is the belief that God exists and is the sovereign authority over the universe. Naturalism is the belief that there is no God and material reality is all that exists. It asserts that science is the ultimate truth. If you can't see it, touch it, observe it or prove it by physical means, it doesn't exist. It is from naturalism that we develop the belief that there is no absolute truth or objective moral standards. Naturalism believes that "morality" is a social construct defined by each person's subjective values and experiences.

If your worldview is naturalism, which means God is not a part of it, you will tend to view morality as relative. You will believe each person interprets their own sense of right and wrong based upon their own beliefs. You will reject the existence of moral absolutes and argue that one's view of morality should never be imposed upon others. In other words, naturalists will tell pro-lifers, "You may think abortion is wrong—and that's fine for you—but don't impose that belief on others. That's 'your truth,' others have 'their own truth' and may feel abortion is necessary and good." Or, to those who oppose gay marriage, the naturalist will say, "You may not believe same-sex marriage is appropriate, but your view is not absolute, that's your morality. Others have the right to believe whatever they want about homosexual marriage."

It is amazing today that many who claim to be Christian, hold to a naturalistic worldview, and do not even realize it. They "believe" in God but reject basic theological doctrines such as the fall of mankind, salvation through Jesus Christ, the justice and wrath of God, and the existence of an eternal hell. They are "Christian Naturalists" who "pick and choose" which doctrines they feel comfortable with. Themes such as forgiveness and God's love are universally accepted but the more difficult truths are rejected as antiquated relics from past generations.

However, if you have a true theistic worldview, then you will believe there is a God, the Bible is His Word and Jesus is the Savior of the World. If this is your worldview, everything in your life will be affected by it. Your philosophies, your politics, your attitudes, your relationships, your parenting, your marriage; in fact, your entire life will be defined by the existence of a Sovereign God.

It must be noted that one's worldview does not develop randomly. It is the result of what we choose to believe about God and how we decide to live in response to that belief. Once our worldview is set, it shapes our opinions, informs our perspectives and determines our course of conduct—essentially it forms our character. This is why the Bible instructs us to be very intentional regarding our worldview.

> Now this I say lest anyone should deceive you with persuasive words... As you therefore have received Christ Jesus the Lord, so walk in Him, rooted and built up in Him and established in the faith, as you have been taught, abounding in it with thanksgiving. Beware lest anyone cheat you through philosophy and empty deceit, according to the tradition of men, according to the basic principles of the world, and not according to Christ. (Colossians 2:4-8)

> I beseech you therefore, brethren, by the mercies of God, that you present your bodies a living sacrifice, holy, acceptable to God, which is your reasonable service. And do not be conformed to this world, but be transformed by the renewing of your mind, that you may prove what is that good and acceptable and perfect will of God. (Romans 12:1-2)

Both texts are addressing the area of our mind and thinking—our worldview. Colossians 2:4-8 says that our minds need to be rooted and built up, established in faith. Why? Because we're surrounded by secular philosophies and belief systems that are "not according to Christ," and are, in fact, hostile to Him. Romans 12:1-2 states we each have a personal responsibility to present ourselves to God for the renewing of our minds. It even says our minds literally need to be renewed. This means our thinking must be transformed from anti-biblical worldviews to a worldview that proves the good, acceptable and perfect will of God.

When the Apostle Paul wrote these words under the inspiration of the Holy Spirit, he was concerned about a pagan worldview dominated by pantheism and spiritism. Those who converted to Christ out of those belief systems needed to be intentional regarding the formation of a new worldview defined by the Word of God.

Today, in western culture, our issue is not so much paganism and spiritism (although these do exist), our concerns are mostly with an amoralistic, naturalist worldview that rejects the authority of God, the canon of scripture and absolute morality. According to Paul, those who convert to Christ must be very deliberate in shifting to a theistic, Christ-centered worldview. For those of us in church leadership, this means being very deliberate in the work of discipleship which helps people to establish God's Word as their moral center. A passage in 2 Corinthians addresses this on an even deeper level: "For though we walk in the flesh, we do not war according to the flesh. For the weapons of our warfare are not carnal but mighty in God for pulling down strongholds, casting down arguments and every high thing that exalts itself against the knowledge of God, bringing every thought into captivity to the obedience of Christ" (2 Corinthians 10:3-5).

This passage reveals that the philosophies of the world are not only around us, but they are also in us. In fact, these attitudes are so ingrained in our thinking, they resist the truth of God. Our minds have been shaped to think a certain way. We may have been raised in homes void of God's Word or trained by teachers and professors who held naturalistic views. Because this is all we know, we hold these positions as truth. In other words, because of your background, you may actually have a worldview that is contrary to the truth of God.

I see it all the time. In my work as a pastor, I encounter people who believe in God and go to church, but when they hear biblical truths such as the depravity of man, the justice of God, the existence of Hell and salvation through Christ alone, they cannot accept them. These truths don't fit into their worldview. What they grew up believing and heard from pop culture runs contrary and resists these truths. It is just as 2 Corinthians 10:3-5 declares, their worldview is like "stronghold" in their minds that "exalts itself against the knowledge of God." As a result, they pridefully resist the truth and say something like, "My Jesus wouldn't do that!" or, "That's not the God I believe in." There's a stronghold in their minds, a belief in a false gospel that is the product of a false worldview that holds them in delusion.

This is why the Apostle Paul says we must "bring every thought into captivity to the obedience of Christ." It's similar to what he said in Romans 12:1-2, do not be conformed to this world but be transformed; and, Colossians 2:4-8 to be "built up in Him and established in the faith." Our worldview, our thoughts, beliefs, and opinions must be surrendered to the truth of God's Word—our minds must be transformed.

FINAL THOUGHTS

What about you? Is your mind being transformed by the Word or conformed to the world? Do you think critically or just accept everything the world tells you? Are entertainers like Oprah and Bill Mahr framing your beliefs? Do you easily agree with Jimmy Kimmel's version of truth or Taylor Swift's hedonistic message of morality? When CNN, MSNBC or Fox News presents their perspectives on abortion, homosexuality, and transgenderism do you just agree that two plus two equals five? Or is your mind being renewed by the truth of God's Word?

Scripture says our major task in life is to discover what is true and to live in step with that truth. It further tells us that the framework for "what is true" is God's revelation to man in scripture, the Bible. Jesus said, "You shall know truth, and the truth shall set you free" (John 8:32). The more our worldview is informed by the principles of God's Word, the wiser and more empowered we become to live overcoming, healthy and fulfilled lives. As well, we will "be ready to give a defense to everyone who asks you a reason for the hope that is in you, with meekness and fear" (1 Peter 3:15).

Pressure Points

three
CREATION AND THE ORIGIN OF MAN

There exists in the scientific community, an intentional and militant bias toward any view that opposes the predominate naturalistic theories of origins. It is a deliberate, predisposed, prejudice against a belief in God, especially among scientific leaders who advocate a naturalist worldview.

Although they knew God, they did not glorify Him as God, nor were thankful, but became futile in their thoughts, and their foolish hearts were darkened. Professing to be wise, they became fools. - Romans 1:21-22

One day a group of scientists came together and decided that mankind had come a long way and no longer needed God. So they selected one from among their group to go tell God they were done with Him. The chosen scientist walked up to God and said, "Listen God, we've decided we don't need You anymore. We can now clone DNA, resolve infertility, change gender, transplant organs and do all sorts of things that used to be considered miraculous. So, You're no longer necessary." God listened patiently and after the scientist was done talking, He said. "Done with Me, huh? How about this: let's have a 'Man Making Contest.'" The scientist answered, "Great, we can do that." "But," God added, "We're going to do this just like I did it back in the old days with Adam." The scientist replied, "Sure, no problem," and he bent down and grabbed himself a handful of dirt. Immediately God interrupted him, and with a thunderous voice said, "No, no, no. Get your own dirt!"

Granted, it's a silly joke, but it demonstrates a tragic reality. Naturalism attempts to explain the mysteries of origins without a

Creator or the truth His Word provides. Genesis 1:1 declares, "In the beginning God created the heavens and the earth." John 1:1-3 states, "In the beginning was the Word...All things were made through Him, and without Him nothing was made that was made." With clear and concise language, the Bible emphatically declares that mankind, and the universe in which we live, was designed and created by Almighty God.

THEISM VS. NATURALISM

There are two predominant worldviews in Western culture today: theism and naturalism. Theism asserts the existence of the God who is the Creator and Sovereign Authority over the universe. Naturalism (or atheism) denies the Creator and insists all things exist as a result of natural, random, chemical and biological processes over billions of years. Where the Bible emphatically declares, "In the beginning God created the heavens and the earth," naturalism says, "In the beginning gases, chemicals, and neutronic particles aligned themselves in a perfect, meticulous fashion and evolved to create our current existence."

Propelled by the Theory of Evolution, naturalism is the prevailing paradigm in western culture today. From an early age, society indoctrinates young minds with secular explanations of a godless existence. It begins with seemingly harmless cartoons like "The Land Before Time" and cute schoolbooks such as "I Used to Be a Fish." Then, as preschoolers mature, they are introduced to people like "Bill Nye the Science Guy" on YouTube, Morgan Freeman on the Discovery Channel, and the compelling animation of Walt Disney. All these influences work together, promoting evolution as though it were an undisputed fact. By the time our youth complete a public education that literally outlaws the mention of God, bans the Bible, and forbids intelligent design, they are well versed in naturalistic theories of origins.

But it doesn't stop there. Naturalism is continually reinforced and sustained in our culture through a steady diet of atheistic theories on television, in pop culture and the media. It's the sacred cow of western society. And if you disagree, if you dare to question this politically correct worldview, you are branded as a science denier and marginalized as an ignorant, deluded, religious fundamentalist.

For the Christian, naturalism has become our modern-day Goliath. If you hold a theistic worldview in this current age of militant secularism, you are just like David confronting the angry giant. Goliath stands there with its arguments and scientific theories. It flexes its muscles and brandishes its data in arrogant defiance trying to intimidate those who trust in the Lord. Ironically, when David spoke against the giant, his brothers scolded him and told him to be quiet. But David would not relent. Instead, he replied, "Is there not a cause?"

This must be our reaction as well. "Is there not a cause?" Is there not a reason to speak up and defend our faith? Is there not a response to the assertions of naturalism and atheistic evolution? My answer—our answer should simply be, "Yes! There is a cause. Yes! There is a reason for the hope that lies within us. There is a truth, a thoughtful and scientific response to defend the biblical claims of intelligent design. We can and should challenge this giant so the testimony of God will stand firm in our culture.

The world will insist, however, that the Theory of Evolution is settled, proven, science. But it is not settled, proven science. We are told that naturalism is the more intelligent worldview; but it is not the more intelligent worldview. We are told that Darwinism and Natural Selection are absolute; but they are not absolute. We are even told that every credible, reliable scientist is a proponent of naturalism and supports evolution; but be assured, that is not the truth!

The truth is there are many, prominent Christians in science and technology today who hold a theistic worldview and regard the theories of creationism as legitimate science. Even the *Huffington Post* (a politically left-leaning publication) admitted this in an article claiming, "A high percentage of scientists that believe in God, or some form of a deity is higher than you may think—51 percent."[1] Among these believers is renowned geneticist Francis Collins who was appointed by President Obama in 2009 to head the National Institute of Health. Dr. Collins is a devout, born again

Christian who has a powerful testimony of his conversion to Christ and boldly declares his theistic views.[2]

In addition, many published lists of Christians in science and technology are easily discovered throughout media and the internet. In fact, one such list identifies one hundred twenty-three prominent leaders in biology, chemistry, physics, astronomy, engineering, earth sciences, and other fields who express faith in a Creator.[3]

Another article titled, "Over 500 Scientists Proclaim Their Doubts About Darwin's Theory of Evolution" provides a collective statement from scientists who assert, "We are skeptical of claims for the ability of random mutation and natural selection to account for the complexity of life. Careful examination of the evidence for Darwinian theory should be encouraged."

For more examples, check out *In Six Days: Why 50 Scientists Believe in Creation* by John F. Ashton and *How Now Shall We Live* by Charles Colson. Both books offer testimonies from contemporary scientists who question the Theory of Evolution and support the advancement of Intelligent Design.

This is significant. It suggests that if you look beyond what the mainstream scientific community claims, if you will research and study for yourself, you will find that not all scientists agree with, nor support, the theories of naturalism. In fact, many insist that arguments to support naturalistic origins and The Theory of Evolution as the only credible science are not accurate. Additionally, there is much science that has been ignored and even withheld because it contradicts what the secularized scientific community—and western culture wants to believe.

For this reason, it is important to define three major errors existing in the naturalistic worldview today. They are (1) the militant bias of naturalism, (2) the implausible basis of evolution, and (3) the denial of intelligent design. By examining these closely, we can understand how the rejection of creationism along with the wide-scale acceptance of atheistic evolution has pulled our society into a culture of delusion and moral decay.

ERROR #1:
THE MILITANT BIAS OF NATURALISM

There exists in the scientific community, an intentional and militant bias toward any view that opposes the predominate naturalistic theories of origins. It is a deliberate, predisposed, prejudice against a belief in God, especially among scientific leaders who advocate a naturalist worldview. Of course, this should not surprise us as Romans 1:21 speaks of those who would "become futile in their thoughts, whose foolish hearts would be darkened. Professing to be wise, they would become fools."

In his book, *The Collapse of Evolution*, Scott Huse writes: "Scientists are human beings too. The effects of prejudice and preconceived ideas, the influence of strong personal convictions, influence them as much as anyone. Many scientists and teachers are unbelievers in biblical Christianity. These factors play an extremely important role in the widespread acceptance of the evolutionary theory."[4]

Patrick Glynn is the Associate Director of George Washington University. He is a summa cum laude graduate of Harvard College who studied at Cambridge University on a Henry Fellowship and also holds A.M. and Ph.D. degrees from Harvard University. Dr. Glynn said, "The fact that so many scientists are willing to accept wild speculations about unseen universes for which not a shred of observational evidence exists suggests something about both the power of the modern atheistic ideology and the cultural agenda of many in the scientific profession. The mainstream scientific community has in effect shown its attachment to the atheistic ideology of the random universe to be in some respects more powerful than its commitment to the scientific method itself."[5]

Perhaps the greatest tragedy of this "militant bias" is that it has infiltrated our education systems. In 1995, the National Association of Biology Teachers (NABT) declared in their position statement on evolution that "all life" is the outcome of "an unsupervised, impersonal, unpredictable, and natural process." The words "unsupervised" and "impersonal" indicate that the NABT has determined, beyond any scientific doubt, that God did not create and has no influence in the universe, in the world, or in mankind. Even more, it implies that an intelligent creator does not even exist, and any belief in such a being is ignorant and misinformed. This bold statement was approved by the NABT Board in March 1995 and was published in 1996 in NABT's journal, and in NCSE's *Voices for Evolution* (2nd Edition).[6]

But such a bold statement left many in the scientific community with unease. If scientific conclusions require empirical proof through repeatable, observational processes, how can anyone claim with absolute certainty that God was not involved in the formation of life? Answer: They cannot. They can only speculate and hypothesize. It's only when one is driven by extreme bias that they justify such absolute statements.

This extreme bias in the NABT was confirmed when, two years later, they were forced to drop the words "unsupervised" and "impersonal" from their statement because it exposed their prejudice and revealed a blatant atheistic, naturalistic position. Any credible scientist understands that one cannot state, in any absolute sense, that life is the outcome of "impersonal" and "unsupervised" processes because such statements cannot be proved scientifically.[7]

Without question, these events revealed an agenda in the scientific community that extended into the education system. They did not, however, abate the momentum that already existed. In 2005, the landmark US District Court Case, *Kitzmiller v. Dover Area School District,* ruled that creationism and intelligent design were religious teachings that violated the separation of church and state and therefore could not be taught in public schools. Naturalism had gained a stronghold in culture. Creationism would never again see the inside of an American public classroom thus securing the atheistic indoctrination of future generations.[8]

So pervasive, so obvious was this bias in the scientific community, that David Berlinski, one of the world's leading physicists who was also an agnostic bordering on atheism, started to raise serious objections. Alarmed by the pretentious scientific conclusions of Richard Dawkins' book *The God Delusion*, Berlinski wrote his own book entitled, *The Devil's Delusion: Atheism and its Scientific Pretensions*. In it he states:

> Has anyone provided a proof of God's inexistence? Not even close. Has quantum cosmology explained the emergence of the universe or why it is here? Not even close. Have the sciences explained why our universe seems to be fine-tuned to allow for the existence of life? Not even close. Has rationalism in moral thought provided us with an understanding of what is good, what is right, and what is moral? Not close enough. Has secularism in the terrible twentieth century been a force for good? Not even close to being close. Does anything in the sciences or in their philosophy justify the claim that religious belief is irrational? Not even ballpark. Is scientific atheism a frivolous exercise in intellectual contempt? Dead on.[9]

It should be emphasized, David Berlinski is not a Christian. He is not a believer in God nor is he an advocate for intelligent design. So why would he write this? He wrote it because he was infuriated by the lack of integrity in the scientific community. He was troubled that the proponents of atheistic evolution and naturalism were just that: advocates and defenders of a worldview, not objective scientists trying to get at the truth.

This bias against creationism is further seen when we consider the second error of the naturalistic worldview: the implausible bases of evolution.

ERROR #2:
THE IMPLAUSIBLE BASES OF EVOLUTION

Genesis 1:21, 25 and 27 tell us, "God created great sea creatures and every living thing that moves; God made the beast of the earth according to its kind, cattle according to its kind, and everything that creeps on the earth according to its kind; [and] God created man in His own image; in the image of God He created him; male and female He created them."

The Naturalistic Worldview insists all life formed accidentally, by random chemical processes and then evolved, without God.

However, such a view is mathematically, statistically, and astronomically improbable (practically speaking, it is impossible). Essentially, evolution insists that certain proteins and amino acids (essential to the formation of life) randomly appeared in primordial slime and perfectly aligned themselves to form DNA which, in turn, became a living cell. Then, through the passage of time and natural selection, this cell evolved into various species of animals and then into humankind.

But the question must be asked. what is the likelihood, or the probability, that the essential amino acids, needed to create life, would be in just the right place, at just the right time, and line up in just the right manner to form DNA and spark the emergence of a living cell? What is the probability? Science itself says it is so unlikely that it is practically impossible.

Francis Crick, Molecular Biologist, and Nobel Prize recipient in physiology & medicine, who was the co-discoverer of the molecular structure of DNA, wrote: "Suppose that one chain (of DNA) is about 200 amino acids long. The chances of 200 acids being present and lining up in the proper order to form DNA is 10 to the 260th power. 10 followed by 260 zeros.'"[10] It is a number of improbability so high, we don't even have a name for it. It is a statistical impossibility. In fact, it is about the same mathematical probability as a tornado passing through a junkyard and assembling a Boeing 747. Or, it is the same probability of a monkey sitting at a computer, slapping on the keyboard and by chance, typing out a full set of Encyclopedia Britannica. Basically, the chance that life formed on its own, without a Creator, is impossible.

Attempting to account for this improbability, some scientists insist if the universe had enough time, anything could happen. If a monkey types long enough, say billions of years, he may well produce an encyclopedia. This is why Darwinism first insisted that the earth was a few million years old. Then later as more complexity in nature was discovered, the age of the universe was revised to 18 million, then 50 million, then in 1927, 1.6 billion, then 3 billion, then 4 billion, and now the estimate is up to about 4.5 billion. Some "experts" even claim the universe is over 13 billion years old.

Why do scientists continually revise the age of the earth? Because the more they realize the complexity of the natural world, the more improbable it is that it happened by chance. And if it did happen by chance, as they suppose, more time is required. DNA formation needs more time. Evolution needs more time. Natural Selection needs more time. Given enough time, those monkeys will be typing encyclopedias. And to support this conjecture, scientists point to the signs of age seemingly indicated in the earth's geologic time scale or radiometric dating.

But a more feasible and acceptable explanation is found in Creationism. God created the life that exists, and created different species of life, and created the earth with the appearance of age. The geologic time scale may suggest billions of years, but only because God created it that way. It's the same with Adam and Eve. God created them as fully-grown adults. If one were to examine them 5 minutes after they came to exist, the examiner would insist Adam and Eve were at least a few decades old. But they were not; they were newly formed beings, who were created as fully grown adults with all the indications of having existed for decades.

Sir Fredrick Hoyle, renowned astrophysicist and lecturer at Cambridge University, who coined the phrase "Big Bang Theory" also questioned the random formation of DNA. He was not a Christian, nor did he believe in intelligent design, but he found the predominant theories of origins to lack credibility. Hoyle calculated the odds that all the functional proteins necessary for life might form in one place by random events and basically said the probability would be the same as "...if you lined up a billion-trillion (ten with 50 zeros after it) blind people, giving each one a scrambled Rubik's Cube, and finding that all solved the cube at the exact same moment."[11] He went on to say, "Life could not have originated on planet earth, genes and DNA are needed from outside this earth to drive the evolutionary process..." In other words, he insisted there was no way on earth, and no amount of time, which could facilitate the random formation of life. There had to be a designer.

So, where did life come from? From where did DNA originate? According to Sir Fredrick Hoyle, it came from outer space.

It's called the Panspermia Theory and suggests that life on Earth was transported here from somewhere else in the universe. Perhaps it was aliens—or some kind of interstellar space dust. Whatever it was, Sir Fredrick Hoyle believed there was no way life began on earth through random processes.

Yeah, aliens did it. It is a tragic irony that scientists who are hostile toward those who have faith in a Divine Creator can easily have faith in aliens and interstellar dust. Make no mistake, evolution is a faith—it's a belief system. This is why Dr. Ben Carson, a pediatric neurosurgeon and member of the distinguished National Academy of Sciences Institute of Medicine, said during a speech at the Celebration of Creation Conference, "I think it takes a lot more faith to believe in evolution than it does to believe in God."[12]

Why not just believe in a Creator? Because many scientists have a militant bias against the Christian Faith and the Creator. Study the biographies of Isaac Asimov, Stephen Hawkins, Frederick Hoyle, Richard Dawkins and you will discover they did not start out with objective, open minds, searching for objective truth. Rather, they began their study of science with the premise that God does not exist, and from there set out to explain man's origins, and the origins of the universe without any reference to or the possibility of God. Furthermore, this is why Hollywood, the Discovery Channel, National Geographic Channel, and most other educational programs present the Big Bang Theory and evolution as the settled science, they have already rejected God and therefore must explain origins without God.

The truth is, you are not an accidental mass of cells that somehow came together in primordial slime. You are a special creation of God. He called you into existence. He loves you and has a design for your life. Even if you feel empty and without purpose. Even if you were said to be an accident or unwanted by your parents. It wasn't your mother or father who decided your existence, it was God. Despite your mother, despite your father, God wanted you here. Somewhere in eternity past, God had a thought, and that thought was of you. And as soon as that thought entered His mind, He fell madly, passionately in love with you and called you forth into existence that He might know you and care for you and bring you fully into the destiny that He has for you.

ERROR #3:
THE DENIAL OF INTELLIGENT DESIGN

The third error of the naturalistic worldview is the blatant denial of intelligent design. It is a "denial" in the sense that those who remove God from theories of origins must refuse any possibility of controlled, deliberate design in natural order and refute all evidence that supports it.

But in the face of their arguments and debates, the Bible emphatically states, "You alone are the Lord; You have made heaven, the heaven of heavens, with all their host, the earth and everything on it, the seas and all that is in them, and You preserve them all. The host of heaven worships You" (Nehemiah 9:6).

Theism asserts an amazing orderliness in nature. It insists on the existence of an anticipatory design which the random processes of evolution cannot explain. Furthermore, this intricate design supports the existence of a Designer. William Paley, an early Christian apologist, and philosopher said, "The marks of design are too strong to be (denied). Design must have had a designer. That designer must have been a person. That person is God." From this, he developed an apologetic known as "Paley's Watchmaker." It suggests a hypothetical to demonstrate creationism: "If you were to find a watch in the woods, you must conclude it had a designer and creator. The intricate series of parts that work together, springs, the cogs, all suggest a watchmaker. Likewise, if one studies the more complex design found in the natural world, he or she must conclude that there is a world designer."

Indeed, there is an intended, anticipatory design that chance evolution or the random explosions of a "Big Bang" cannot account for. For example, consider the detailed elements of design found on the planet earth and its place in our solar system.

The earth is the perfect distance from the sun, it rotates at the perfect speed, and is tilted at the perfect angle to support life. If it were further away from the sun, all life would freeze. If it were closer, life would burn to ashes. As well, if the earth did not rotate, one side would be permanently facing the sun and would be searingly hot, with the other in permanently frozen darkness. Additionally, the earth is tilted at 23.5 degrees, the perfect angle to provide seasons each year, vital for survival. If the earth was straight up and down, countries further from the equator would have winter all year long and couldn't grow food to sustain life; and countries at the equator would be too hot to be inhabited.

Add to this the design of the earth's atmosphere. It consists of 78% nitrogen and 21% oxygen, the exact amount needed to sustain human and animal life. It also contains an Ozone Layer that protects all living creatures from the sun's ultraviolet rays. The sun's UV rays have so much energy they would kill us immediately. But God anticipated this threat and provided the ozone. Ironically, the Ozone Layer poses a serious problem for human and animal life—it is highly poisonous. If we were to breathe it, we would die instantly. However, God placed it safely away, 10 miles above the earth's surface where it can filter the sun's UV rays without killing us below.

Clearly, God fashioned the Earth and hung it in orbit around the Sun in perfect calculations to support the life He created. There is much more evidence to support this claim, including the orbit of the Moon, its size and gravitational pull, how the Moon controls the ocean tides of the world which are essential to oceanic and coastal life. Then there's the Carbon Cycle (photosynthesis), the Hydrologic Cycle, the Rock Cycle and so many other ecosystems of the Earth.

The more we learn about our planet, the more amazed we are at how extraordinarily well suited it is for life. So specific is this design, it could not have happened through billions of years of happy coincidences. There is a "Divine Watchmaker," the Creator God, as revealed in Scripture:

> For since the creation of the world His invisible attributes are clearly seen, being understood by the things that are made, even His eternal power and Godhead, so that they are without excuse, because, although they knew God, they did not glorify Him as God, nor were thankful, but became

futile in their thoughts, and their foolish hearts were darkened. Professing to be wise, they became fools." Romans 1:20-22

The evidence of intelligent design is not only in the world He created; His signature is upon us, His creations. Consider the miraculous architecture of the human body: the engineering marvel of the eye, the complexities of the ear, the mysteries of the brain, the wonders of human consciousness, the muscular system, the respiratory system, the circulatory system, the nervous system. Truly, the psalmist was correct when he said, "I will praise You, for I am fearfully and wonderfully made; Marvelous are Your works, and that my soul knows very well" (Psalm 139:14). Without a doubt, the intricacies of the human body are far too advanced to be the product of randomly formed DNA, chance evolution and genetic mutation. God designed us. God made us. We are His creations.

The evidence all is all around. There is an amazingly intricate design reflecting the power, intelligence and care of the God who made us and fashioned a planet to sustain us. As Isaiah 45:18 says, "This is what the Lord says—He who created the heavens, He is God; He who fashioned and made the earth, He founded it; He did not create it to be empty, but formed it to be inhabited."

WHY NOT ACCEPT THE SIMPLE TRUTH OF A CREATOR?

Clearly, the culture in which we live is predominately naturalistic. Having eliminated God from the equation, prominent scientists and educators, together with media and pop culture, have formulated their explanations of origins and philosophies of life without any reference to the Divine. Rather than embracing the existence of a Creator who both loves them and holds them accountable, they prefer illusions of magical explosions that bring order out of chaos, aliens who deposit DNA, and species that evolve into complex organisms through an infinite number of perfect mutations.

It begs the question: Why? Why offer these bizarre explanations of bewildering complexities? Why try to hide the simple truth that God created it all? Why indeed? It comes down to one very simple fact. Man does not want God, because man does not want to be governed.

Man wants to be his own master—his own creator. Man wants to make his choices without facing the reality of a God who judges and holds him accountable. Hebrews 9:27 confronts us with this awesome, yet terrible certainty: "It is appointed for men to die once, but after this the judgment."

The three main errors existing in the naturalistic worldview: the militant bias of naturalism, the implausible basis of evolution, and the denial of intelligent design all rise from mankind's greatest turmoil. It is the agonizing truth that "if God is real, I will be held accountable and therefore must allow him to rule over my life." Rebellion in the heart of man cannot allow this and will hold desperately to any rationalization that comforts him in his revolt against the authority of God.

For the Christian living in this age, the truth is clear: God created the universe, the earth and every living thing upon it. Let us not be intimidated by those who have rejected the reality of a Creator. Let us make know our faith in God as we remember the words of the Apostle Paul in 1 Timothy 6:20-21 (KJV):

> O Timothy, keep that which is committed to thy trust, avoiding profane and vain babblings, and oppositions of science falsely so called: Which some professing have erred concerning the faith. Grace be with thee. Amen.

Pressure Points

Pressure Points

four
THE SANCTITY OF HUMAN LIFE

Men and women were created for the specific purpose of reflecting the image of God and existing in relationship with God through communion with His Spirit. This gives every person a dignity that cannot be lost. One's color or ethnicity does not matter. It makes no difference if one is young, old, male, female, American, Asian, African or Hispanic.

There is neither Jew nor Greek, there is neither slave nor free, there is neither male nor female; for you are all one in Christ Jesus. - Galatians 3:28

Shout your abortion?

It began in 2015 when a young woman responded to congressional efforts to defund Planned Parenthood. She made her stand by proudly declaring her recent abortion on social media. Within days, Amelia Bonow's posts went viral, and the hashtag #ShoutYourAbortion, fueled by a supportive news media, became an iconic phrase. Millions of women would soon follow on Facebook and Twitter, not only "shouting their abortions" but declaring they had no regret over ending the lives of their unborn children.

By 2018, the Shout Your Abortion movement became a commercial success. Complete with trendy graphics, savvy marketing and a lucrative clothing line, women around the world were empowered to shout their abortion with slogans such as "Abortion is Freedom," "Everyone Knows I Had An Abortion," and even "Thank God for Abortion." By the end of that same year, the movement released a book aptly titled "Shout Your Abortion." It featured forty-three women from all walks of life who proudly celebrated the death in their wombs.[1]

It was not just a commercial phenomenon. There was a purpose to all the slogans, the marketing, the clothing line, the book, and the social media; they wanted abortion to become a cultural norm. No longer should killing your unborn child be taboo. No longer should there be a stigma or shame attached. Abortion should be "acceptable." It should be "normalized." It should be "celebrated."

At no other time was this demonstrated more profoundly when Michelle Williams stood before the world to give an acceptance speech at the 2020 Golden Globes. Awarded best actress in a limited series, Williams proudly declared that her success could never have been achieved had she not made the choice to terminate an unwanted pregnancy earlier in her life. It was a statement met with resounding applause and lauded by CNN as an "impassioned" and "powerful speech about choice." What was the choice? To put her pursuit of fame and success above that of her unborn baby's life.

It sounds so brave, so courageous—that a woman would abort her baby to be freed from the burden of pregnancy so she could pursue a career. And of course, with the glitz and glamour of Hollywood, it looks so noble, so heroic. But it's all a lie. It's nothing more than the worst kind of idolatry: the worship of self. It is the love of one's pleasure at the expense of most helpless and weak among us—the unborn. It is the height of American hedonism: to serve self and sacrifice anything—or anyone who is a threat to our selfish pursuit. Tragically, like so many lies in our culture, this "choice" promises fulfillment but leaves us empty and broken.

Leslie Blackwell serves as a co-regional coordinator for *The Silent No More Awareness Campaign*, which aims to expose and heal the pain of abortion. She shared her abortion story in an interview for *National Review Magazine*.[2] As a college senior in 1980, while landing a job as a broadcast journalist, she discovered she was pregnant. "Next thing I knew," she said, "I was going to get rid of this 'inconvenience.' I've got a big career to get to." Leslie had an abortion, but it was nothing to shout about. As stated in her online testimony, "I stayed in bed for a day or two, bleeding and crying, feeling hollowed out."[3] Regarding the Shout Your Abortion Movement, Leslie Blackwell says, "I think that they're absolutely delusional, because any woman that's been through an abortion experience will tell you it's not a piece of cake. It hurts, you cry, you feel hollowed out, you are absolutely broken. It haunts you. You'll never forget that day."[4]

It's called the sanctity of human life. God created life and gave us an inherent sense of its value. When life is discarded as an inconvenience through abortion or cheapened by society through euthanasia, it devalues all of us. We all feel less significant and less valued. That inherent sense of worth and value, given to us by our Creator is marred and diminished. Life feels empty and lost, as though it doesn't matter and has no purpose.

This is where the church, as salt and light, must rise with a voice of hope and meaning. Life is sacred! Life is valuable! Life is a creation of God given to us to be celebrated and protected. Shout your abortion? No! Shout your creation! God created you, gave you purpose, cares for you and holds in the sovereign will of His loving, caring hand.

LIFE IS SACRED

There are three overarching biblical truths that frame our thinking on the issue of the Sanctity of Human Life. First, God created human life to be sacred. Second, God is sovereign over the life He created. Third, God forbids the murder of the life He created. Understanding each of these truths empowers our message of life in this culture of death.

TRUTH #1:
GOD CREATED HUMAN LIFE TO BE SACRED

The word "sacred" means "sanctified" or "set apart for a specific purpose." It is a term used to describe something that is uncommon and singular in nature and use. It is why we use the phrase "Sanctity of Human Life" when referring to this truth. Human life is sacred because every human is created in God's own image. We do not exist as through a chance collision of chemicals in primordial slime that mutated over billions of years and evolved into persons. Nor do we exist as the mere result of biological processes in a human uterus. We exist because there is a Creator who designed us, created us, loved us, called us forth and gave us purpose.

Genesis 1:27 tells us "God created man in his own image, in the image of God he created him." Genesis 5:1-2 says "In the day that God created man, He made him in the likeness of God. He created them male and female and blessed them and called them Mankind in the day they were created." Mankind—human life—was created in a distinct way, for a distinct purpose, through a distinct means and is "sacred." Human life stands in a category all by itself.

Animal, insect and plant life are also beautiful and amazing creations of God, but we do not call them sacred. They are in a different category than human life because they are not created in the image of God. In fact, they are gifts to us, given by God to sustain and enrich us. My wife and I have a dog named Max. We love him. He's a part of the family, but we understand that his life is not the same as human life. As cute and cuddly as he may be, Max was not created in the image of God. Max was created by God for the enjoyment and benefit of our family. The same is also true for other animal life such as fish, fowl and four-legged creatures used for man's consumption.

But man is different. When God created man, it was much more personal and intimate. Genesis 2:7 tells us "And the LORD God formed man of the dust of the ground, and breathed into his nostrils the breath of life; and man became a living being." God used this same intimate care in creating woman: "And the LORD God caused a deep sleep to fall on Adam, and he slept; and He took one of his ribs and closed up the flesh in its place. Then the rib which the LORD God had taken from man He made into a woman, and He brought her to the man" (Genesis 2:21-22).

Men and women were created for the specific purpose of reflecting the image of God and existing in relationship with God through communion with His Spirit. This gives every person a dignity that cannot be lost. One's color or ethnicity does not matter. It makes no difference if one is young, old, male, female, American, Asian, African or Hispanic. As Thomas Jefferson wrote in the Declaration of Independence, "All men (and women) are created equal (and) are endowed by their Creator with certain unalienable Rights." It's why Paul wrote in Galatians 3:28: "There is neither Jew nor Greek, there is neither slave nor free, there is neither male nor female; for you are all one in Christ Jesus."

This is also why there can be no tolerance of racism, bigotry or ethnic supremacy of any kind in the Body of Christ—or mankind in general. If you believe that your ethnic group or the color of your skin gives you some superiority, you don't understand the sanctity of human life. No race is superior to any other. No people group is greater than another. All are created in the image of God, equally loved and valued by God, to serve His distinct purpose.

This sacredness of all human life also extends to every person, regardless of his or her mental state or physical form. Those who are severely disabled, mentally ill, or wracked with pain from a terminal illness, still bear the image of God and are endowed by their Creator with certain unalienable rights. All human life is sacred, regardless of condition, color, age or ethnicity.

TRUTH #2:
GOD IS SOVEREIGN OVER THE LIFE HE CREATED

The word "sovereignty" means "having absolute authority and without accountability." It implies one can do as he wishes and is not under anyone's power or control—nor does he answer for any choices he makes. This means God has absolute authority over my life, your life and every life He created. It further means that because He alone is sovereign over life, that He alone, as the Creator, establishes the boundaries for when life begins and ends, not me or you.

James 4:14 says life "...is a vapor that appears for a little time and vanishes away." Obviously, death is certain for every sacred life. However, God alone controls when and how a person's death occurs. Hebrews 9:27 tells us, "It is appointed for men to die once..." and Ecclesiastes 8:8 says, "No one has power over the time of their death" (NIV). God reserves for Himself the final say over death. He determines when life begins and ends for every human. He alone has that authority. Euthanasia, suicide and abortion are man's unjust attempts to usurp that authority from God.

TRUTH #3:
GOD FORBIDS THE MURDER OF LIFE

It's called the Sixth Commandment, and it states emphatically, "You shalt not murder" (Exodus 20:13). It's important to note that some versions of scripture, like the King James Version, use the term "kill" instead of "murder." Unfortunately, the term "kill" does not capture the full nuance of the Hebrew meaning. The actual Hebrew word refers to the specific act of unlawfully terminating innocent, human life—the act of murder.

This is an important distinction to make because there are several exceptions in Scripture where God permits, even orders, His people to take the lives of others. One example is in Genesis 9:6 when speaking of law enforcement and capital punishment: "Whoever sheds man's blood, by man his blood shall be shed; for in the image of God He made man." After the fall of man, it was imperative for God to establish certain laws to maintain justice and order in society. The sinfulness of man had to be kept in check by certain legal consequences for heinous acts. Murder would result in the loss of the murderer's own life. Absent this consequence, mankind would descend into chaos. Ecclesiastes 8:11 warns, "Because the sentence against an evil work is not executed speedily, therefore the heart of the sons of men is fully set in them to do evil."

Another exception is the taking of human life in the context of war. This is explained in a doctrinal treatise by Saint Augustine entitled "Just War Theory." Referencing Romans 13:4, Augustine claims that God has given the sword of justice to the government for the purpose of protecting peace and punishing wickedness. He insisted that Christians living in a fallen and corrupt world would be required to oppose evil through physical force when authorized by a legitimate authority.

One more exception to the prohibition of killing is when one takes another's life in an act of self-defense. Exodus 22:2 tells us,

"If the thief is found breaking in, and he is struck so that he dies, there shall be no guilt for his bloodshed." This precept is demonstrated in what many states call the "Castle Doctrine." It is a rule of law that gives a person the right to use deadly force when defending his home, property, life or the life of another. The particulars of this doctrine vary from state to state, so it is advisable to research how your state applies it, if at all.

EUTHANASIA AND SUICIDE

While there may be exceptions to the sixth commandment, nowhere in scripture is there an ethic to support euthanasia, physician-assisted suicide or suicide.

Suicide is the act of deliberately and purposefully causing one's own death. Physician-assisted suicide occurs when a medical professional provides the means of suicide (e.g. medication) which a patient takes of his or her own volition. In euthanasia, the physician directly and intentionally causes death. Nowhere does Scripture condone or make any allowance for any of these life-ending means.

These are different from what we know as a DNR. A "Do Not Resuscitate" order is a prewritten, legal order used in terminal cases in which a person has indicated they do not want to receive heroic measures, such as CPR or breathing machines, if their heart stops beating. A DNR (also known as a Living Will) is different from suicide or euthanasia which are active means through which someone intentionally ends their life. A DNR is a passive means. It is a simple directive that predetermines treatment (or the withholding of such) in terminal cases. The signer is indicating their desire to allow death to come naturally, as appointed by God, without providing life-saving measures.

Essentially, euthanasia and suicide violate the Sanctity of Human Life by usurping God's sovereign control over the end of life. He created life to be sacred. Advocates of euthanasia, suicide, and physician assisted suicide are defying God's sovereignty by saying, "I am my own authority. No God will direct my life or control my death. The time and means of my death are my own matters and may be initiated by me. I will be sovereign over me and God will not take that sovereignty from me."

Obviously, this is a difficult and highly controversial issue. Great care and compassion need to be exercised when encountering families and individuals grappling with end of life issues. For more information, read *Ethics for a Brave New World* by John and Paul Fienberg.[5]

ABORTION

Perhaps no issue has become more divisive, controversial and painful in the United States than that of abortion. Not only have millions of unborn children been subject to the pain of pregnancy termination, so have the millions of women (and men) who have lived through it. Even years later, many are still suffering the remorse and sadness which often follows this painful event.

The tragic reality is that one in four women will have an abortion in their lifetime. Those who haven't, probably know someone who has. Abortion is everywhere. Sadly, most (if not all) of those who've had abortions are left with a profound sense of loss and regret from the experience. For many, it is a loss that stays with them for the rest of their lives. This is true, not only for women but also for the men who've suffered as well. Abortion is a tragedy that impacts everyone it comes into contact with.

Because of this, the conversation about abortion should be approached with sensitivity and compassion. If you or someone you know had gone through this experience, please understand that nothing in these pages is intended to deepen the pain you feel or condemn you for the decisions you've made. Most women who have had abortions are victims themselves. They have been manipulated by an industry and deceived by a culture that has convinced them that terminating a pregnancy was a noble and healthy option. It is a lie and, tragically, many have believed it.

Thank God that the grace He offers through Jesus Christ can cleanse you of your guilt and offer life restoring forgiveness. The cross provides redemption—especially from the sin of abortion. In Christ, there is no condemnation and you can rise from your regret knowing God loves you, accepts you, and offers you a future and a hope, filled with peace. Having said that, there is no way to sugar coat the reality. Abortion takes the life of an innocent human being. And millions of innocent lives hang in the balance. The regrets of our past cannot prevent us from speaking truth to the present, and hopefully effecting change for the future. As Christians, we must speak truth to culture.

According to the World Health Organization, 40 to 50 million abortions occur around the world annually, which is about 125,000 abortions per day. In the United States, we terminate approximately 900,000 pregnancies per year, which means every day, 2,400 unborn children are murdered.[6] Since Roe vs. Wade was passed in 1973, over 50 million unborn children have been ripped from their mothers' womb, and it's not getting better.[7]

As of this writing, in New York State, there are 218 abortion providers who perform over 105,000 abortions every year. This translates to 288 infant murders everyday.[8] Tragically in January 2019, New York Governor Mario Cuomo signed into law the Reproductive Health Act which opens the door for abortions to occur up until the time of birth.[9] As well, during an interview in 2019, Governor Ralph Northam voiced support for a similar bill proposed in his state in which he endorsed "after-birth abortion." This is nothing less than state-sanctioned infanticide.[10]

Abortion is a cultural pressure point for the church, one that we cannot remain silent on because when the church unites in its effort to resist evil, society will be impacted. In upstate New York, residents of the Town of Carmel, petitioned their local town board to pass a resolution urging its state legislature to repeal the Reproductive Health Act and protect the life of the unborn. It was an initiative that began with Christians, was vocally backed by Christians and consequently, was adopted by the Town of Carmel Town Board. Although state legislators have not yet repealed the RHA, this demonstrates what it means to be salt and light in the world. When the church raises its voice, it can make an impact, it can affect change, it can be a force for good and stay the rise of evil.

This is what the salt and light is supposed to do. This is the church impacting culture. It happened in England with the abolition of slavery and again in the United States with the Emancipation Proclamation. It occurred in Hitler's Germany when Christians withstood Nazi policies to exterminate the Jews, and again and again with many other righteous causes championed in society by the church. As stated in a quote attributed to Edmund Burke, "The only thing necessary for the triumph of evil is for good men to do nothing." The church is to be light and salt—a force for good, staying the advance of evil, murder and injustice in the world.

THE CORE ISSUE OF ABORTION

When it comes to the issue of abortion, all our objections and arguments come down to one over-arching biblical ethic: from the moment of fertilization, that organism which has been conceived is a "human life." It is a distinct, separate life, the direct offspring of its human parents with its own, distinct human DNA, different from the mother, different from the father, uniquely created with its own purpose and destiny. And this is the point that organizations such as Planned Parenthood and other abortion advocates must reject because if the life in the womb is human, it is entitled to the same rights and protections as any human being. This is why most abortion advocates insist that what is in the womb is not a human life.

In May of 2019, Christine Quinn, a board member at the *National Institute of Reproductive Health*, said on CNN, "When a woman gets pregnant, that is not a human being inside of her. It's part of her body and this is about a woman having full agency and control of her body and making decisions about her body."[11] The argument goes like this: the unborn is "a part of the mother's body, like an internal organ. If a woman needs to remove her appendix or tonsils, that's an issue of privacy, she should be free to do with her body, what she wants. This is the foundation upon which the "pro-choice" movement rests, women will say, "It's my body, my choice."

But the biblical position could not disagree more. When an abortion occurs, it is not simply the removal of some part (or tissue) from the mother's body. What is being aborted is a life that is distinct from, and other than, the mother's life. It is a separate organism with its own DNA, its own functional system, its own cellular growth. It is an established, unique human life. Psalm 139:13–16 says, "For You formed my inward parts; You covered me in my mother's womb. I will praise You, for I am fearfully and wonderfully made; Marvelous are Your works, and that my soul knows very well. My frame was not hidden from You when I was made in secret... Your eyes saw my substance, being yet unformed. And in Your book they all were written."

Without question, what is in the mother's womb is more than a mere clump of cells or an appendage like an appendix or tonsils. The Bible emphatically declares that it is a human life, created by God. As such, it is sanctified, set apart, and uniquely crafted in His image. It is a life that is sacred.

The word of the Lord came to Jeremiah and said, "Before I formed you in the womb, I knew you; before you were born I sanctified you; I ordained you a prophet to the nations" (Jeremiah in 1:4–5). Clearly, God is telling Jeremiah that he was set apart and called prior to his body being fully formed. It means Jeremiah was a person—a human life—in the womb; and before his birth, God had purpose, meaning and destiny for him.

This is not merely a biblical assertion. There is a preponderance of expert testimony and scientific evidence concluding that the unborn life in the mother's womb, from fertilization, is human life. Even more, most of this testimony comes from non-Christian, proabortion, naturalistic scientists.

The standard medical text, *Human Embryology and Teratology*, written by Embryologists Ronan O'Rahilly and Fabiola Müller, states "Fertilization is a critical landmark because a new genetically distinct human organism is thereby formed."[12]

Pro-choice philosopher Peter Singer, in his book *Practical Ethics*, wrote "There is no doubt that from the first moments of its existence an embryo conceived from human sperm and egg is a human being."[13]

Dr. Louis Fridhandler, in the medical textbook *Biology of Gestation*, says fertilization is "...that wondrous moment that marks the beginning of life for a new unique individual."[14]

Dr. Keith Moore and Dr. Keith Persaud's textbook, *The Developing Human: Clinically Oriented Embryology* says, "Fertilization is the beginning of a human being."[15]

The 4th chapter of Scott Gilbert's book, *Developmental Biology*, is simply titled: "Chapter 4: Fertilization: Beginning of a New Organism."[16]

In other words, based on these statements of fact, provided by experts in their field, the organism in the womb is not an appendage of the mother's tissue, it is not cellar growth attached to the mother, it is not an organ of the mother, or cell's belonging to the mother. Of course, it is in the mother, but it is a new, separate, living organism with human DNA, often having a different blood type than the mother, different chromosomal makeup than the mother, and is a completely different human life than that of the mother.

Doctors E. L. Potter and J. M. Craig, in *Pathology of the Fetus and the Infant*, wrote: "Every time a sperm cell and ovum unite a new being is created which is alive and will continue to live unless its death is brought about by some specific condition."[17]

If that's not enough, consider the following quotes from the United States Senate Judiciary Committee that invited some of the world's most prominent scientists and physicians to testify on the question of when life begins. All of the quotes from the following experts come directly from the official government record of their testimony.[18]

Dr. Alfred M. Bongioanni, professor of pediatrics and obstetrics at the University of Pennsylvania, stated, "I have learned from my earliest medical education that human life begins at the time of conception.... I submit that human life is present throughout this entire sequence from conception to adulthood and that any interruption at any point throughout this time constitutes a termination of human life.... I am no more prepared to say that these early stages [of development in the womb] represent an incomplete human being than I would be to say that the child prior to the dramatic effects of puberty...is not a human being. This is human life at every stage."

Dr. Jerome Lejeune, professor of genetics at the University of

Descartes in Paris, the discoverer of the chromosome pattern of Down syndrome stated, "When fertilization has taken place a new human being has come into being." He stated that this "is no longer a matter of taste or opinion," and "not a metaphysical contention; it is plain experimental evidence." He added, "Each individual has a very neat beginning, at conception."

Professor Hymie Gordon of the Mayo Clinic said, "By all the criteria of modern molecular biology, life is present from the moment of conception."

Professor Micheline Matthews-Roth from Harvard University Medical School testified, "It is incorrect to say that biological data cannot be decisive. ...It is scientifically correct to say that an individual human life begins at conception. ...Our laws, one function of which is to help preserve the lives of our people, should be based on accurate scientific data."

Dr. Watson A. Bowes, of the University of Colorado Medical School, said, "The beginning of a single human life is from a biological point of view a simple and straightforward matter—the beginning is conception. This straightforward biological fact should not be distorted to serve sociological, political, or economic goals."

This truth, this one truth alone, defeats the pro-abortion, pro-choice argument. What exists in the womb of the woman's body is a living human organism, a human life. And if it is a human life, it deserves to live, to be defended, protected, and preserved. That unborn human life has "The Right to Life." It is a right asserted, not only on biblical authority, but also on U.S. Constitutional authority.

This truth was overwhelmingly affirmed in July 2000 by the U.S. House of Representatives when they unanimously passed "The Innocent Child Protection Act," a bill making it illegal to execute a pregnant woman. The logical reason for this decision is that a preborn child is an individual person, distinct from his mother and with his own separate right to life.[19]

When does life begin? When it comes to scientific testimony, the United States government, scientific evidence and the Word of God, life begins at fertilization, what we call conception.

A NEW TWIST TO AN OLD LIE

Unfortunately, as pro-abortion advocates are forced to concede the reality of human life at fertilization, they are shifting their argument. Rather than protecting that life, they seek to justify—on moral ground—the necessity of killing it. "It may be human life," abortionists argue, "But it's not true personhood. It's a 'lesser' form of human life." By dehumanizing the unborn and categorizing them as inferior, they feel justified in denying them the rights they deserve.

During a debate with Trent Horn on the topic of abortion on March 13, 2014, Professor Cecili Chadwick of California State University San Marcos stated, "What I am arguing today is not whether or not the fetus is human or whether or not the fetus is alive. It's been proven. It's indisputable the fetus is alive, and the fetus is human. The question today is 'should abortion be legal?' And I am answering that question, 'Yes.'"[22]

In an article in the *New Republic,* Naomi Wolf, a prominent feminist and author, admonished fellow abortion supporters to be forthright on this issue when quoted: "Clinging to a rhetoric about abortion in which there is no life and no death, we entangle our beliefs in a series of self-delusions, fibs, and evasions. And we risk becoming precisely what our critics charge us with being: callous, selfish and casually destructive men and women who share a cheapened view of human life. ... [We] need to contextualize the fight to defend abortion rights within a moral framework that admits that the death of a fetus is a real death."[21]

Feminist Camille Paglia is even more blunt: "I have always frankly admitted that abortion is murder, the extermination of the powerless by the powerful. Liberals, for the most part, have shrunk from facing the ethical consequences of their embrace of abortion, which results in the annihilation of concrete individuals and not just clumps of insensate tissue."[22]

It's an amazing admission. Many abortion advocates no longer deny that abortion murders a human life. They readily admit that what is killed is alive and human—and they embrace it. What they will not concede, however, is that this human has a right to live.

To rationalize their killing of the unborn, abortionists attempt to offer justification. In the afore mentioned debate, Professor Chadwick stated there are plenty of circumstances in which one has the right to kill human life. She then explained it is not wrong to kill someone who is threatening your life, or to kill people in war, nor is it wrong to kill through state sanctioned executions. Seriously? Is it reasonable to compare a helpless, innocent baby in the womb to an enemy combatant or a convicted criminal? Of course not. Criminals and combatants are free-thinking individuals who have made deliberate choices to become threats; a baby in the womb has made no such choice and is completely undeserving of death. This failed logic merely exposes the futile attempt to justify what is unjustifiable.

As these arguments deteriorate, pro-choicers must resort to redefining the unborn as a "non-person" or "a lesser form of human life." In doing so, they insist that these "lesser" humans are not entitled to the same rights as the mothers (the "full humans") who carry them. It's a new twist to an old lie.

For those who study history, this argument is familiar. It is the same rationale slave owners used regarding their slaves. It's the same logic Jim Crow laws used to discriminate against African Americas. It's what the Nazis said about Jews. It's what one empowered, dominate class of humans will always say to justify subjugating, enslaving and euthanizing a weaker class: "They are less than human and not entitled to the same rights that we have."

Survivors from the Holocaust say, "Never Again!" But "never again" is happening again. As Georg Wilhelm Friedrich Hegel said, "What we learn from history is that we do not learn from history. Experience teaches us that people and governments have never learned anything from history or acted on principles deduced from it." David Livingstone Smith, in his book *Less Than Human: Why We Demean Enslave and Exterminate Others*, reminds us that during the Holocaust, Nazis referred to Jews as vermin, the genocidal Hutus in Rwanda called Tutsis cockroaches and throughout history, slave owners regarded slaves as subhuman animals. Today, in western society, history is repeating itself. We have dehumanized an entire class of fellow humans for widespread discrimination and genocide. And tragically, it's the most vulnerable among us—our unborn children.[23] Today, in modern America, abortion is infanticide. And future generations will condemn us in the harshest terms.

Let's be clear. Not only is the organism in the womb human life, it is fully and completely human. Of course, it is not fully developed, but it is wholly human with its own DNA, its own functional system, its own cellular growth, identity, destiny and future ordained by God. It is an established, sacred, human life and must be respected, protected and given the right to live.

When abortionists categorize underdeveloped human life as less human and then justify killing it on those grounds, they are standing on a slippery slope that opens a very dangerous door. Firstly, it puts every newborn child in peril. Even after a child exits the birth canal, he or she is still significantly "underdeveloped." Their brains are underdeveloped, their motor skills are nonexistent, their sense of autonomy and personality have yet to be established. Would not these millions of children be candidates for "termination" by those like Governor Ralph Northam who supports "after-birth abortion." Would this not provide a slippery slide to state-sanctioned infanticide? Secondly, what about the millions of people with birth defects, missing or incompletely formed limbs, impaired mental capacity, or have lost significant body functions? Do politicians and doctors get to decide that they are less than human and therefore not entitled to human rights? Where does it end?

This is why we defend the "Sanctity of Human Life." It is not the "sanctity of fully-formed bodies" or the "sanctity of complete mental capacities." It is the sanctity of life. When human life is present, it must be treated as sacred and entitled to the rights every human enjoys, regardless of body type, mental acuity, developmental completeness or sentient autonomy.

FINAL THOUGHTS

Abortion is murder. It is the killing of innocent human life. It is one of the greatest evils man has perpetuated on his fellow man. To classify human life in the womb as less than human and then to reach into that womb with metal instruments, tear it apart, suction it out and discard it as waste is an unthinkable evil that will mark our culture as one of the most brutal and heinous in mankind's history. Based on data from the Guttmacher Institute, along with information from the Centers for Disease Control, the National Right to Life Education Foundation reports that almost 61 million unborn American children have been murdered in the womb since the passage of Roe vs. Wade in 1973.[24] This is a national tragedy!

Tragic as it is, our anger should not be directed toward the individuals who sanction and perform such evils. These are lost people simply doing what lost people do, being led by the darkest impulses of their fallen nature. We should not be angry at them any more than salt should be angry at meat for rotting and putrefying. That's what meat does, it rots. If blame is to be placed, it should also be put on the salt for failing to be a preserving influence. That's what salt does—or at least what it's supposed to do. The same applies to light. It would be foolish for a man to rail against the darkness when he holds an unlit flashlight in his hand. In fact, he is more to blame for not allowing his light to shine. This is exactly the point Jesus was making in Matthew 5.

> You are the salt of the earth; but if the salt loses its flavor, how shall it be seasoned? It is then good for nothing but to be thrown out and trampled underfoot by men. You are the light of the world. A city that is set on a hill cannot be hidden. Nor do they light a lamp and put it under a basket, but on a lampstand, and it gives light to all who are in the house. Let your light so shine before men, that they may see your good works and glorify your Father in heaven. (Matthew 5:13-16)

The salt needs to act as salt. The light needs to shine as light. Salt prevents rotting. Light dispels darkness. We must do more than argue against abortion, we must be a positive influence—a force for good—so the world can see our good works and glorify the God who calls us demonstrate them.

First, the church must actively support institutions that offer counsel and support to women who are pregnant (and the men that care for them). Almost every city in the US has crisis pregnancy centers that offer women options beyond abortion. Churches in those same cities should partner with them. Financial support, volunteer support, prayer, and vocal support are only a few ways local congregations can offer their partnership.

Second, the church should encourage adoption and foster care. The sad reality is that many impoverished women, who are unmarried and lacking resources, are seeking abortions. They become pregnant and feel they have no better alternative than to terminate their pregnancy. They cannot see how they will care for and raise a child—especially if they currently have children. These women need to know that there are many loving families praying for the blessing of children but unable to conceive themselves. The woman with the unexpected pregnancy could be the answer to their prayer. The church could be a tremendous resource in connecting these families together in the miracle of life.

Third, the church must offer support and aid to mothers who give birth to children and need assistance in raising their children. Too many churches persuade struggling women to keep their unborn children and then offer no help to them after the children are born. Pastors and churches must be proactive in assuring mothers to be that they are not alone. They must be reminded that there is a loving community of people who are there to offer care and support when needed.

Lastly, pastors and church leaders must not remain silent on this issue. Speaking out against abortion, teaching the biblical doctrine of the Sanctity of Life, empowering their congregations to stand firm on these issues and raise their voices in society is essential. An excellent resource for equipping ourselves in this debate is Randy Alcorn's book *Pro-Life Answers to Pro-Choice Arguments*.[25] With great detail, Alcorn exposes the myriad of rationale used by abortionists to support their position and offers intelligent responses.

Pressure Points

five
PROMISCUITY AND MARRIAGE

A lack of clarity on the biblical ethic concerning premarital sex has led many to develop "their own" sexual ethic—an ethic that allows for sex between consenting partners outside of marriage.

Flee sexual immorality. - 1 Corinthians 6:18

In his letter to the believers at Corinth, Paul issues the clear directive to "Flee sexual immorality." See 1 Corinthians 6:13-20. It seems simple to understand, but in today's highly sexualized culture, in which the overwhelming majority of adults are sexually active, restraining one's sex drive seems ridiculous. To most people, sex is a natural craving that should be appeased; it's an appetite of the body like "food for the stomach." If your body craves it (the world would say), satisfy the craving. Go for it. If it feels good, do it.

The data bears this out. In studies published by the Guttmacher Institute[1] and Public Health Reports,[2] data was analyzed on sexual and marital behaviors in American culture. The results showed the vast majority of Americans had sex before marrying. Specifically, the surveys revealed by age 20, 75 percent of young men and women had premarital sex, and by age 44, 95 percent of men and women had premarital sex. They further revealed that among those who abstained from sex until at least age 20, 81 percent had unmarried sex by their mid-40's. Clearly, sexual promiscuity has become a norm in our culture. In fact, in a 2015 paper entitled, "Changes in American Adults' Sexual Behavior and Attitudes," Jean M. Twenge, of San Diego State University, reported that from the 1970s to present day, acceptance of unmarried sex has grown considerably. In the early 1970s, 29 percent of Americans believed that premarital sex was "not wrong at all" compared to 62 percent of millennials today. In fact, data shows that 45 percent of today's millennials engage in casual sex with a first date or a "pickup."[3]

Of course, it's hardly a new revelation that American culture is overtly sexual and saturated with promiscuity. Anyone with a television, computer or cellular device can potentially be exposed to a barrage of sexual content every day. What is surprising, however, is how many "Christians" consume this content on a regular basis and are sexually active. In fact, we are witnessing a strange phenomenon in the church today, called "The New Christian Sexual Ethic."

Relevant Magazine, a Christian publication, recently published an article entitled "(Almost) Everyone's Doing It" by Tyler Charles. Based upon research conducted by the National Campaign to Prevent Teen and Unplanned Pregnancy, Charles claimed that young adults between the ages of 18 and 29, who identify as evangelicals, are no less sexually active than their non-Christian counterparts: 80% of Evangelical Singles are having sex outside of marriage.[4] Reinforcing this claim, Brandon Robertson in his article "Rethinking Sex," cited the same source material but offered an interesting explanation. He writes, "This lack of Biblical clarity (on premarital sex) has led many in the millennial generation to develop a new Christian sexual ethic—an ethic that allows for sex between consenting and committed partners outside of marriage. And this new sexual ethic isn't a small trend—a surprisingly large number of committed Christian young people have adopted this position and are engaging sexually with their significant others."[5] He goes on to explain that young evangelicals are sexually active, not because they have forsaken God, but because sex is a matter of conscience and not clearly defined Biblical morality. Robertson further states, "Is sex before marriage a sin? Potentially. But that is between each individual, their significant other, and the Lord."

This is a direct contradiction of God's Word. Anyone with a basic understanding of scripture knows the command of the Apostle Paul in 1 Corinthians is absolute: "Flee sexual immorality."

This is not a personal conviction that each one decides for himself; this is a Biblical command. It is clear, unambiguous and repeated throughout the New Testament. 1 Thessalonians 4:3-5 states, "For this is the will of God, your sanctification: that you should abstain from sexual immorality; that each of you should know how to possess his own vessel in sanctification and honor, not in passion of lust, like the Gentiles who do not know God." Ephesians 5:3-5 says, "But fornication [meaning sex outside of marriage] and all uncleanness or covetousness, let it not even be named among you, as is fitting for saints; for this you know, that no fornicator, unclean person, nor covetous man, who is an idolater, has any inheritance in the kingdom of Christ and God."

In each of these scriptures, as well as Paul's command in 1 Corinthians 6:18, the Greek word for sexual immorality is "porneia." Porneia is the broadest term for sexual sin in the Greek language and refers to any form of sexual activity between two individuals who are not united in a heterosexual marriage. It means if you are sexually active, and that person with whom you are sexually active is not your husband or wife, then you are committing "porneia," sexual immorality—and it is sin. To be clear, the act of sex is not immoral, it is the act of sex outside of marriage that is immoral. Hebrews 13:4 tells us, "Marriage is honorable among all, and the bed undefiled; but fornicators and adulterers God will judge."

To fully grasp the prohibition against "porneia" or "sexual immorality," it is necessary to clarify the concept of "immorality." "Morality" is an objective standard of right and wrong, defined by the Word of God. To have a "Biblical Worldview" is to embrace the notion of objective morality. It is to believe in God, and that God has created certain "life laws" and principles by which we are required to live. Those principles are the foundation for appropriate conduct and behavior, the basis of morality. When it comes to sex, God has shown us its proper use: sex is for a man and a woman in the context of heterosexual marriage. Anything outside of that is inappropriate, it is immoral. This is not open for discussion or debate. This is not for speculation or personal opinion. This is not relative to each person's own subjective view of right and wrong. It is a matter of principle, the principle for human sexuality that the Creator has established in His Word.

WHAT IS IT ABOUT UNMARRIED SEX THAT MAKES IT "IMMORAL?"

Unmarried sex is immoral simply because it violates God's designed purpose for human sexuality. But why? 1 Corinthians 6:13 states, "Now the body is not for sexual immorality but for the Lord, and the Lord for the body." Verses 19-20 further state, "Do you not know that your body is the temple of the Holy Spirit who is in you, whom you have from God, and you are not your own? For you were bought at a price; therefore, glorify God in your body and in your spirit, which are God's." This simply means our bodies are not our own, but we are a temple of the Holy Spirit, a place in which God dwells in order to have a relationship with us, to fulfill His purposes—even as it relates to our sexuality. In other words, our sex drive does not exist for our personal gratification, to be satisfied with anyone to whom we are attracted. Our sex drive exists for a purpose that God has designed—that primary purpose being marriage.

1 Corinthians 6:16 tells us, "Do you not know that he who is joined to a harlot is one body with her? For "the two," He says, "shall become one flesh." The purpose of sex is for making "the two" into "one flesh." Sex is an ability God has given to man and woman, as a means to consummate the joining of themselves into a union of oneness.

The secular world sees sex as a carnal appetite, a craving to satisfy for one's own gratification. But Paul is saying that God created sex to consummate the whole-life commitment (the two shall become one flesh), and to express that "united-oneness" for the duration of that lifelong union. When we misuse sex, we are abusing it (which is an act of immorality) and causing the Holy Spirit (who is in us) to be a participant in that immorality.

Sex is reserved for that one person with whom you wish to become one flesh. Sex is not something you give away to just anybody, it is not a cheap thrill to steal in the backseat of a car with anyone you think is cute. This devalues sex into something cheap and vulgar. Sex is not to be cheapened. It is meant to be one of your most precious and valuable abilities reserved for a sacred covenant. It is a gift God gave to you, to share with that one person in marriage, which expresses to that one person that you are giving up your independence and joining yourself to that person's life—not just physically, but emotionally, spiritually, mentally, and legally. Sex is not a cheap thrill, it is a valuable, sacred offering.

In fact, when one misuses or abuses his or her sexual ability, Paul says it is a sin against one's own body (1 Corinthians 6:18). It's a curious statement because other activities, such as drug abuse, smoking or suicide could be noted as worse sins against one's body. But Paul emphasizes porneia—why? Because when you surrender yourself sexually to a person, who has not pledged himself or herself to you in marriage, you are devaluing and degrading the means of commitment God has given you for the express purpose of the marriage covenant. You have sinned against your own body.

COMMON ATTITUDES TOWARD UNMARRIED SEX TODAY

Moral relativism is the belief that all morality is relative. In other words, there is no absolute standard for right and wrong that applies in every context. Circumstances and each person's subjective experience determines whether something is right or wrong to do. Perhaps nowhere is this demonstrated more than in the area of sexual promiscuity.

The following are five common attitudes or excuses people give for engaging in unmarried sex today. Each one is not based upon an objective standard of right and wrong, but by what people have decided is right for themselves. Unfortunately, these attitudes are not limited to non-Christians but are also found in many churched people.

The first attitude is *"Unmarried sex is not wrong if we love each other."* This may sound romantic, but the Bible makes no distinction between "loving" and "unloving" sexual relations. The only biblical distinction is between married and unmarried people.

According to Genesis 1:28, sex within marriage is blessed, and according to 1 Corinthians 7:2–5, sex outside of marriage is "fornication" or "sexual immorality." It is a sin. is not blessed. And love has nothing to do with it.

The second common attitude says *"Times have changed. What was immoral in biblical times is acceptable today."* Based on this rationale, we should determine morality based upon popular opinion. If something has become a norm in society, then we should adjust our morality to accept it. But how would that apply to Taliban culture in Afghanistan where stoning women to death for allegations of adultery are a cultural norm? What about stealing? That's pretty popular. In fact, prisons are filled with people who believe stealing should be normal. What about lying? Studies show that most people lie every day, multiple times. Maybe lying should be taken off the list of sins, too. And then there's adultery and covetousness? What about murder? The reality is times may have changed but sin is still sin and will always be sin. The issue is not how you or I feel about morality, or what culture says is acceptable, the issue is how God views it. And God's character does not change with culture. Malachi 3:6 says, "I am the Lord, I do not change."

The third attitude says, *"Whether it is sin or not doesn't matter. I love Jesus and Jesus loves me despite how I live."* Of course, Jesus loves us. He died on the cross to prove that love. But can one truly say he or she loves Jesus while continuing in those things God clearly says not to do? Does one who really loves God willfully commit acts that are offensive to Him, thus provoking His wrath upon His own Son as a penal substitution? This is the same rationale a foolish husband uses when he says, "I love my wife, despite the fact I beat and abuse her and sleep around with other women." Any sane person would respond to say "No! Absolutely not! You do not love your wife, and your actions prove it."

This is exactly what is meant in 1 John 2:3-4: "Now by this we know that we know Him, if we keep His commandments. He who says, 'I know Him,' and does not keep His commandments, is a liar, and the truth is not in him." In other words, "Talk is cheap." Simply "saying" you love Jesus has little meaning; what matters is that you align your conduct with the love you profess to have. In Matthew 7:21-23, Jesus said, "Not everyone who says to Me, 'Lord, Lord,' shall enter the kingdom of heaven, but he who does the will of My Father in heaven. Many will say to Me in that day, 'Lord, Lord, have we not prophesied in Your name, cast out demons in Your name, and done many wonders in Your name?' And then I will declare to them, 'I never knew you; depart from Me, you who practice lawlessness!'" Again, remember Hebrews 13:4: Marriage is honorable...but fornicators and adulterers God will judge." Here's the bottom line: saying you "love Jesus," does not give cover to commit unmarried sex. In fact, our love for our sin speaks a far louder message than our professed love for Jesus.

The fourth attitude toward unmarried sex is *"We're married in God's eyes. We don't need a piece of paper to prove our love."* Marriage is not something we merely fabricate into existence by wishing it to be so. Marriage is a covenant relationship defined by God, established when two people pledge themselves, through specific vows of commitment, witnessed by community, in an act of consecration before God. This requires a proper authority to ensure that the union is blessed by God and aligned with God's Word. This requires a proper pledge that identifies the commitments and vows being made. This requires a public affirmation, a ceremony with witnesses so everyone knows that you are now married and have exchanged rings as a sign of your marital pledge. This requires a legal approval to ensure you are credible persons, with legitimate identities, joined in a legal, fiduciary manner.

The fifth attitude is the claim of cohabitation. It says, *"Living together is a practical alternative to marriage."* This is a major pressure point in the church today. According to the National Center for Family and Marriage Research, 66 percent of married couples live together before marriage. While this may be more typical with non-Christian couples, cohabitation is becoming more commonplace in the church.

THE CRISIS OF COHABITATION

Guiding couples who live together without marriage is an issue the church cannot avoid. Church leaders must not remain silent and need to teach the ethic of marriage from a biblical perspective. This is especially true as more and more young people are being indoctrinated by the world and experimenting with cohabitation. The following are three lies and three truths that expose the dangers couples face when they move in together without first being married.

The first lie is that *"Living Together is the new norm; marriage is outdated and unnecessary."* Studies show that 4 out of 10 Americans think marriage is obsolete and 45 percent of men and women believe it's heading for extinction.[6] This is an unfortunate paradigm in a naturalistic worldview. As people move further and further away from faith in God, they lose sight of the virtues espoused in the Bible regarding the marriage covenant.

God created marriage for a reason. It was to establish the ethic of mutual commitment between husband and wife and to the family unit. Cohabitation, by its very definition, requires no commitment. It's a relationship with a backdoor—an "escape hatch" if things don't go as expected. This is why many couples avoid marriage; they want to keep the option to leave the relationship at any time, no strings attached. "If I'm unhappy, or if I get bored, or if we're not compatible, I can simply leave. You go your way and I'll go mine."

This is a horrible way to build a relationship. In fact, it's a weak foundation that will collapse at the first sign of stress. There is no motive for perseverance. There is no fortitude to work through the hard issues. There is no discipline to deny self, control anger, seek resolutions, work towards forgiveness, or persist through disappointment and pain.

By contrast, these are the exact qualities that the act of marriage establishes and that results in lifelong relationships. In fact, this is what love is all about. Love is not a feeling; it is not an emotion. Love is an act of the will. It is a decision. In 1 Corinthians 13, the "Love Chapter" of the Bible, love is defined as long-suffering, choosing to be kind, bearing through difficulty, believing the best in a person and remaining faithful through disappointment. Relationships can be hard, but it is the commitment to fidelity, established in marriage, that holds couples together.

The second lie is that *"Living Together saves money and provides financial benefits."* This is the foremost reason for cohabiting in the US. Obviously, one household is less expensive to maintain than two. So, young adults who want to live independently from their parents and can't afford it, get a roommate. Often this roommate will be a romantic partner. Other cohabiters avoid marriage because of the financial benefits many states offer to single parents. In New York State, single parents can receive over $1,000 per month in cash and food subsidies as well as medical assistance. If they marry, they lose those benefits. One woman I interviewed in the process of her seeking to be water baptized was resolute in not marrying her live-in boyfriend: "I can't get married because I will lose my single-mom benefits." Even though she claimed to be a Christian, she was lying to the state about living alone as single mother while also sleeping with a man she had not married, all for financial benefits. I explained to her that she was living in sin and must decide if she wants the blessings of New York State or the blessings of God. Sadly, she chose New York State. Although welfare has helped many struggling families, it is undermining marriage and rewarding cohabitation. Unfortunately, I could not baptize her or her live-in boyfriend. Baptism is a sign of repentance and walking in new life in the Lordship of Jesus Christ. People who are living together in sin have not repented, nor are they surrendered to the Lordship of Christ.

The third lie is that *"Living Together allows us to test our compatibility before we marry."* I hear this a lot, but it simply is not true. The reality is you and your partner are not compatible! Every relationship is made up of two sinners: two people who are selfish by nature, want to do things their own way, have their own needs, and come with high expectations for one another. That is a recipe for incompatibility. What makes two people compatible is not a personality assessment or six months of premarital counseling. What makes a couple compatible is standing before God at an altar, pledging their lives to one another and exchanging vows to love, honor and cherish each other in sickness and in health, in poverty and in wealth, for better or for worse, until death do they part—and then keeping the vows! It is commitment that makes us—that forces us—to be compatible. It is the bond of marriage that holds a couple together.

My wife and I have been married for over thirty years. Certainly, we had shared values that made us seem "compatible," but it was not some notion of "compatibility" that kept us together, it was our commitment, our vows of marriage. Truth be told, we were often more combative than we were compatible. We disagreed, we argued, we offended each other. There were times we didn't like each other; times we wanted to leave—this is what happens in relationships. But what kept us together was our vow to God. It was the commitment to marriage that made us say: "Whatever the cost, whatever it takes, we're going to make this marriage work." And by God's grace (through the marriage covenant) we raised five kids and sustained over thirty years of marriage—joyfully. Had we merely been "living together" to "test our compatibility," we would have never made it past the first year.

Exposing the lies about cohabitation is not enough, we must also tell the truth about it. There are harsh realities that many couples face after choosing to move in together. Unfortunately, in a naturalistic culture that denies the value of biblically-based principles, these truths are rarely addressed. In fact, the world will insist that cohabiting leads to a successful marriage, but the data proves otherwise.

The first truth is that *"Living Together increases the likelihood of infidelity in a relationship."* Generally speaking, cohabiting individuals are less committed to their partners and are more likely to have sexual encounters outside their current relationships.[7] In fact, in an article entitled *"Unmarried Couples 'More Likely to Cheat'"*, it was reported that only 43 percent of cohabiting men claimed to be faithful to their partners compared with almost 90 percent of married men. As well, 20 percent of cohabiting women admitted to being unfaithful compared to 4 percent of married women.[8] Furthermore, *The Journal of Marriage and Family* reported the odds of infidelity are more than twice as high for cohabiters than for married persons. Couples who live together before marriage raise the odds of marital infidelity by 39 percent.[9] Marriage makes a difference—a huge difference.

The second truth is that *"Living Together often leads to breakup or divorce."* Glen Stanton, in his book *Why Marriage Matters*, states "The expectation of a positive relationship between cohabitation and marital stability has been shattered in recent years by studies indicating that those who cohabit before marriage have substantially higher divorce rates than those who do not. In fact, the recorded differences range from 50 percent to 100 percent higher."[10] In an article entitled, *The Role of Cohabitation in Declining Rates of Marriage*, the data shows that 40 percent of cohabiting relationships will disrupt before marriage, and marriages that are preceded by living together have a 50 percent higher disruption rate than marriages without premarital cohabitation.[11] Another study showed that over 60 percent of couples who live together before marriage will never marry, and of the 40 percent that do marry, 5 out of 6 will be divorced within 3 years.[12]

The third truth is that *"Living Together brings a litany of adverse, toxic effects into a relationship."* To name a few: cohabiting leads to sexual promiscuity which results in 44 percent of cohabiting women with unintended childbirths. Cohabiting couples report more fighting and violence and less reported happiness than married couples. Cohabiting individuals have higher levels of depression and substance abuse, compared to married persons. Cohabiting couples earn less money and are less wealthy than their married peers later in life.

Hard to believe? Do some research. A quick study will reveal a wealth of information substantiating these claims. Living together does not enhance, improve or enrich one's life or relationship. It has a greater likelihood of producing misery, pain, disappointment and regret.

A FINAL WORD

Why does cohabitation ruin relationships and undermine happy marriages? Because living together is sexually immoral and provides a poor foundation for a lasting commitment. By its very definition, cohabitation is an arrangement of convenience. It requires no commitment and cannot sustain the challenges that are certain to come with any relationship. Cohabitation is not marriage; it is not God's plan for establishing a family and will never be blessed by God.

The good news is God wants to bless you and your relationship. He wants to put His grace upon your life and shower you and your partner with His goodness. If you're cohabiting, but you desire to bring yourself under His blessing, take steps now to solidify your relationship through marriage. The grace of God is waiting for your surrender. The best is yet to come, but you must submit to His perfect will.

Pressure Points

Pressure Points

six
HOMOSEXUALITY AND GENDER

Our culture has accepted two huge lies. The first is that if you disagree with someone's lifestyle, you must fear or hate them. The second is that to love someone means you must agree with everything they believe or do. Both are nonsense. You don't have to compromise convictions to be compassionate. - Rick Warren

Have I therefore become your enemy because I tell you the truth? - Galatians 4:16

It's entirely possible that you can love someone while at the same time disagreeing with them. In fact, if you believe someone is making an unhealthy or immoral choice, it is an act of love, not only to express your disagreement but to warn that person of the dangers ahead.

No one understands this truth better than parents. Parents love their kids. They accept their kids. But they do not always agree with them or approve of the choices they make. Parenting involves a thousand difficult conversations, often centered on disapproval but motivated by love. Because they care deeply for their children, moms and dads regularly confront their kids' unhealthy behaviors, explain their disagreement and try to persuade them appropriately. This is all occurs while loving them unconditionally.

Today there are two major social issues that require the church to demonstrate this same kind of "tough love": homosexuality and transgenderism. Unfortunately, our culture now interprets the church's efforts to speak the truth in love as an act of hateful bigotry. There are even attempts to legislate the church into silence. In June 2019, the California State Assembly adopted Bill ACR 99 which calls on religious leaders and others with "moral influence" to affirm homosexuality and transgenderism as acceptable and normal lifestyle choices. Furthermore, it condemns biblically-based, therapeutic efforts to help people with unwanted same-sex attraction or gender confusion as "ineffective, unethical and harmful." Homosexuality and transgenderism are becoming firmly rooted in our culture.[1]

We are also seeing it in the church as denominations such as the Episcopalians, Lutherans, Presbyterians, Quakers, and others are now sanctioning same-sex marriage and the homosexual lifestyle. It's a constant theme in pop culture, entertainment, social media, and politics. CNN recently aired a 2019 LGBTQ Town Hall in which democratic presidential candidates touted their pro-gay and transgender agendas, promising to reengineer American culture to suit their extreme views. One candidate even stated his belief that churches and religious institutions should lose their tax-exempt status if they did not support same-sex marriage. Even more concerning is the LGBTQ agenda that has actually become part of the curriculum in certain public-school districts and universities. Today, schools, churches, and children are being constantly pressured to embrace homosexuality and transgenderism as normal and acceptable lifestyles—all in the name of "love."

As pressure continues to mount, it is imperative that church leaders—and Christians in general—speak clearly and directly to the issues. The time for vague ambiguity has passed. We need leaders who are both courageous and compassionate, concerned more with impacting culture than preserving their popularity.

THE BIBLICAL PRINCIPLES OF HUMAN SEXUALITY

Let's be clear, neither the Bible, the church, nor true followers of Christ are anti-gay, anti-trans or anti-anybody. The Bible teaches that people matter to God—all people. Regardless of lifestyle choices or sexual preference, every person is God's special creation whom He values and desires a relationship with.

In the church I have pastored for over 30 years, our doors have always been open to people of all backgrounds, beliefs, ethnicities, and (yes) sexual orientation. In fact, we have had people of same-sex attraction attend our services, participate in our programs, and enroll their kids in our school, all while receiving love, care, and ministry from our pastors. So, any accusation that we are bigots, homophobes, or haters of gay people, is simply not true. Having noted this, it is also true that we challenge all people, homosexuals and heterosexuals alike, to live out the principles of sexuality taught in the Scriptures.

The first principle is God created sex and called it good. Genesis 1:27-28 tells us, "God created man in His own image... male and female He created them. Then God blessed them, and God said to them, 'Be fruitful and multiply [and] fill the earth.'"

The second principle is God created sex for heterosexual marriage. In Matthew 19:4-5, Jesus said: "Have you not read that He who made them at the beginning 'made them male and female,' and [He] said, 'For this reason a man shall leave his father and mother and be joined to his wife, and the two shall become one flesh'?" Furthermore, Hebrews 13:4 states, "Let marriage be held in honor among all, and let the marriage bed be undefiled, for God will judge the sexually immoral and adulterous." God created man. He then created woman, and then created marriage. After they were married, they had sex—and God called it good.

This means, if you are in a biblically defined heterosexual marriage, God intends for you to have sex. He thinks it's good. However, every sexual act outside of a biblically defined marriage is outside of God's plan, and it is not good. This includes premarital heterosexual sex, extramarital heterosexual sex, and all homosexual sex—whether married or unmarried.

The third principle is clear. There is absolutely no affirmation of homosexual activity, same-sex marriage, or the gay lifestyle anywhere in Scripture. Homosexual activity is sin, plain and simple. However, is not a special sin, it is not a super-sin. It is sin, just like any other sin—just like heterosexual activity outside of marriage is sin, just like adultery is sin, just like pornography is sin.

Nevertheless, the Bible is clear on the issue of homosexuality. Starting in the Old Testament, Leviticus 18:22 says, "Do not have sexual relations with a man as one does with a woman; that is detestable." Lest that be misunderstood, it is restated in Leviticus 20:13: "If a man has sexual relations with a man as one does with a woman, both of them have done what is detestable." Note how the word "detestable" is used in both verses. It is a powerful descriptive that indicates God's extreme displeasure with this specific sin.

Some will undoubtedly say, "That's Old Testament. We're living in the New Testament; we're in the age of grace." This is true, but sin is still sin and the New Testament affirms this.

In Paul's Epistle to the Romans, he addresses a culture that has rejected the authority of God and worships carnal pleasures and sexuality over God. Romans 1:26-27 states: "For this reason God gave them up to vile passions. For even their women exchanged the natural use for what is against nature. Likewise, also the men, leaving the natural use of the woman, burned in their lust for one another, men with men committing what is shameful, and receiving in themselves the penalty of their error which was due." Clearly, Paul is identifying both male homosexuality and female lesbianism as practices God condemns.

In Paul's letter to the Corinthians, he is equally clear. The city of Corinth was notorious for its sexual immorality. It was a crossroad of commerce that had become known for its debauchery and sexual lewdness. As a local church had been planted there, Paul wanted to remind the congregation about God's moral order. "Do you not know that the unrighteous will not inherit the kingdom of God? Do not be deceived. Neither fornicators, nor idolaters, nor adulterers, nor homosexuals, nor sodomites, nor thieves, nor covetous, nor drunkards, nor revilers, nor extortioners will inherit the kingdom of God" (1 Corinthians 6:9–10). Note that Paul specifically mentions homosexuals and sodomites in verse nine. The Greek terms used are specific to male homosexuals in both active (male) and passive (feminine) roles.

In writing to Timothy, Paul identifies homosexuality as a lifestyle that is contrary to sound doctrine. "The law is not made for a righteous person, but for the lawless and insubordinate, for the ungodly and for sinners…for fornicators, for sodomites, for kidnappers, for liars, for perjurers, and if there is any other thing that is contrary to sound doctrine" (1 Timothy 1:9-10). Paul is unambiguous in his use of the word "sodomites." He is referring to those who participate in homosexual activity.

These passages make it clear that homosexual behavior violates God's plan for human sexuality. Sex was designed by God for use between a male and a female in a heterosexual marriage. Sex was never intended for homosexual activity. This is why it is called "sin." Whenever one does something that violates God's plan or His intended order, it is defined as sin. This is not one man's opinion. This is not a church or denominational opinion. This is God's Word and His word is the final authority.

BORN THAT WAY?

There are many today who reject this standard for human sexuality by parroting an objection touted by many in pop media and secular culture: "How can God call it sin? Aren't homosexual people 'born that way?'" More to the point, people refer to the notion of a "Gay Gene" that pre-programs people for same-sex attraction. If that's true, one may argue, how could homosexual activity be a sin if people are naturally born gay?

The idea of a gay gene was put forth in a 1992 *Newsweek* magazine article titled *"Is This Child Gay?"* based upon a few studies that included gay twins and brain tissue from homosexual men, this article suggested the possibility that people are born with a genetically gay predisposition, a "Gay Gene." Eventually, *Time* magazine picked the story up, followed by the *Wall Street Journal*, the *New York Times,* and National Public Radio. It wasn't long before almost every media outlet was reporting that people are gay because of a gene that programs their sexual preferences organically. Even today, many years later, we are still hearing it.

The problem with this theory is that modern science, now over twenty-five years later, boldly and unequivocally states that there is no such thing as a "Gay Gene" nor is there any empirical proof that a person is born gay. In 2017, The American Psychological

Association issued this statement: "There is no consensus among scientists about the exact reasons that an individual develops a heterosexual, bisexual, gay or lesbian orientation. Although much research has examined the possible genetic, hormonal, developmental, social and cultural influences on sexual orientation, no findings have emerged which permit scientists to conclude that sexual orientation is determined by any particular factor or factors."[2] Furthermore, in 2016, a Johns Hopkins University School of Medicine report stated: "While some people are under the impression that sexual orientation is an innate, fixed, and biological trait of human beings—that, we are 'born that way'—there is insufficient scientific evidence to support that claim."[3] Additionally, the National Association for Research and Therapy of Homosexuality Institute stated that certain hormonal factors, when mixed with certain environmental conditions, may affect sexual orientation, but "There is no such thing as a 'gay gene' and there is no evidence to support the idea that homosexuality is simply genetic."[4]

Science is clear: there is no "Gay Gene" or DNA code that predetermines sexual orientation. While there may be certain hormonal or environmental factors that predispose a person, the idea that God made people gay is simply not true. Any attempt to advance this argument is an exercise in confirmation bias based upon outdated junk science.

But, for the sake of argument, let's suppose a genetic link to homosexuality does exist. My response would be, so what? Studies have suggested a genetic link to alcoholism, drug addiction, pathological violence, and even to heterosexual promiscuity. But are we willing to excuse those behaviors on the basis of "my genes made me do it!"? Absolutely not. All this would prove is that we are all born broken and messed up. We are all sinners, "born that way." Romans 5:12 says, "Through one man [Adam] sin entered into the world, and death through sin, and so death spread to all men, because all sinned." Every one of us has inherited the sin virus. For some people that virus makes them inclined to alcoholism or to substance abuse or violence or promiscuity; it could even mean some people are inclined toward homosexuality. If true, however, it's not because God created them that way, it's because of the twisted inclination of our nature toward sin.

But the good news of the gospel is this: regardless of the sin tendency you inherited, Christ died for you, so you can be set free from sin. 2 Corinthians 5:17 tells us, "If anyone is in Christ, he is a new creation; old things passed away; all things become new." Despite what California law says, the LGBTQ movement, or the predominate view of pop culture, Jesus still sets souls free from sin—this includes homosexuality or any sin that has a person in its grip.

TRANSGENDERISM

There is a second sexuality issue which is also becoming a pressure point for the church: transgenderism. Although many are not as familiar with this as they may be with homosexuality, it has become a cultural phenomenon that western culture is fixated upon.

Transgender is an umbrella term for the condition of expressing a gender identity that does not match a person's biological and genetic sex at birth. It is when a genetic male feels more comfortable presenting as a woman, or a genetic woman feels more comfortable presenting as a man. It may mean dressing in a way that expresses one's preferred gender, it may involve hormonal treatment to align one's physiology to that gender, it could even include surgical treatment that alters one's body to match their "felt gender."

To fully grasp the meaning of transgenderism, we need to understand that the transgender community believes there is a difference between one's biological sex and one's gender identity. In this school of thought, the term "sex" refers to one's biological make up (male or female) as determined by his or her chromosomes and primary sex characteristics. By contrast, the term "gender" or "gender identity" refers to one's internal, subjective sense of what he or she is sexually. This may be male, female or somewhere in between, on a gender spectrum. In other words, biologically you could be a male, but emotionally, you feel like a female. The result is you would present yourself in a female role and take steps to alter yourself physically despite the fact you were born with male chromosomes and a fully functioning male body. Psychology calls it "Gender Dysphoria." It is a disconnect between one's biological make up and his or her emotional identity that produces mental distress.

To be clear, transgenderism is when someone alters their physical appearance or changes their body to portray their "preferred gender." It's the belief that I can determine my own gender, based not on biology, but in defiance of biology. It's the notion that I can have every biological characteristic of a male, but if I say I am female then I am female and should expect society to accept the gender I prefer, despite my true sexual, biological identity.

For example, Katelin Jenner previously identified as Bruce Jenner. Bruce Jenner is a man—or was a man. We know this because he was a gold medal Olympic athlete who competed in male events. Bruce had every biological characteristic of a male. He had all the chromosomes of a male. He had all the body parts of a male. But because Bruce "felt" more comfortable as a female, he decided to call himself a female. And society—that includes you and me—are expected to accept Bruce (now Katelin) as a female. We are expected to use his female name, his female pronouns and regard him—or her—as perfectly normal. And if we don't, we are branded as bigots who have no compassion for transgender people.

But there is a hard, brutal reality. You can call Bruce a female. You can treat Bruce like a female and give Bruce a female name and access to everything a female should have, but Bruce is still a man. His "feelings" have nothing to do with it. It's biology, plain and simple. He has male chromosomes, male DNA and male body parts. God created him to be a man and he will always be a man—whether he "feels" that way or not.

Please forgive me if this sounds callous or insensitive. There is no intent to mock or minimize the pain that many with gender dysphoria suffer. Words cannot adequately convey the agony that these precious souls—and their families—must endure. They should be treated with sincere love and genuine compassion.

Unfortunately, what is a profound psychological dilemma for

many hurting souls has morphed into an aggressive, radical agenda for social justice warriors. Transgenderism has become a political sport. Politicians use it to advance their careers. Pop stars and Hollywood elite use it to signal their "woke virtue." Militant activists use it to position themselves as cultural powerbrokers. Sadly, the dysphoric who suffer are mere pawns in someone else's agenda and culture is being torn apart.

Just read the newspaper, or see it dominating social media platforms. Headlines and media outlets feature stories of males transitioning to females and being given access to girl's locker rooms. Teenage girls are transitioning to men, seeking hormone therapy and surgically altering their bodies. Male athletes are competing in women's sports, winning women's trophies and receiving women's scholarships. In New Jersey, a family can have their children removed if they do not support a child who wants to transition. In New York City, teachers, health care providers, and employers are required to use the preferred pronouns of trans-people and can be fined up to $250,000 if they do not. Social media platforms, like Facebook, now offer to seventy-one gender options. And if you refuse to support someone's dysphoria by using their "preferred personal pronouns," be ready for an all-out attack on your character, your faith, your family and your integrity.

THE BIBLE AND GENDER

But while culture has been twisted into confusion the Bible provides clarity and truth, especially concerning human sexuality and gender. The first truth is that one's gender is not a subjective choice; it is an unchangeable reality that God predetermines for each person.

Scripture tells us that when God created mankind, he created two sexes: male and female. Genesis 1:27 says, "So God created man in His own image; in the image of God He created him; male and female He created them." There is nothing in the Bible to indicate a spectrum of gender, or the option to change one's gender. (While there may be rare exceptions of intersex births, these do not apply to the issue of transgenderism. Transgenderism typically involves an individual whose gender is clearly defined and then chooses to transition to the opposite gender.)

When God created mankind, he created individuals to be either male or female. This identity is not based on how one feels or some subjective notion of which gender one prefers to manifest. It is based on biology—plain and simple. When a baby is born, the gender—the sex—is known and identified. The idea of "gender identity" as being distinct from biological sex is an absurdity. It is a fabrication of politically correct science gone wild. Gender and sex are the same thing. How one feels about their gender is another issue altogether and should potentially be treated as a cognitive disorder (in fact, this was how it was treated until 2013*).

Is it true that someone may feel dysphoric about their gender? Certainly. There are men that struggle with their masculinity and women who struggle with their femininity. They feel uncomfortable in the gender God gave them. They feel insecure about who they are and long for a different identity. Such is the reality of our broken humanity. But the fact that they are emotionally uncomfortable with their sex, doesn't mean they can just decide to no longer be male or female. Life doesn't work that way—and neither does science.

In 2015, Dr. Paul McHugh stated: "Transgendered men do not become women, nor do transgendered women become men. All they become are feminized men or masculinized women, (including Bruce Jenner). They become counterfeits or impersonators of the sex with which they 'identify.'"

Many would-be outraged by that statement so it's worth noting that Paul McHugh is one of the most esteemed psychiatrists of our time. He serves as the Distinguished Professor of Psychiatry at Johns Hopkins Medical School and was the former psychiatrist-in-chief at Johns Hopkins Hospital. He goes on to write: "In fact, gender dysphoria—the official psychiatric term for feeling oneself to be of the opposite sex—belongs in the family of similarly disordered assumptions about the body, such as anorexia nervosa and body dysmorphic disorder. Its treatment should not be directed at the body as with surgery and hormones any more than one treats obesity-fearing anorexic patients with liposuction. The treatment should strive to correct the false, problematic nature of the assumption and to resolve the psychosocial conflicts provoking it."[5]

IT IS A THINKING DISORDER, NOT A BODY DISORDER

This brings us to the second biblical truth regarding transgenderism. Gender dysphoria is not a "body disorder," it's a "thinking disorder."

Jeremiah 17:9 says, "The heart is deceitful above all things, and desperately wicked; who can know it?" The worst advice you'll ever receive is, "Follow your heart." It's bad counsel—especially when one's heart is out of sync with their gender. The Bible tells us we cannot trust what our heart tells us, or what our thoughts want us to believe. In fact, this why so many are depressed and defeated. Instead of talking to themselves, they are listening to themselves. They accept the confusing chaos of their own delusion instead of pulling down strongholds and bringing every thought captive to the obedience of God's Word.

At the risk of oversimplifying the issue, this is similar to how a young woman with Anorexia and Bulimia may suffer. Regardless of how thin a young woman may be, she "feels" fat. Her mind keeps telling her, "You're overweight. You can't eat. You need to purge." We know the problem is not with her body, the problem is with her mind. She has a thinking disorder. We would never tell that young lady, "Well, if that's how you feel, then you must be too fat. You should starve yourself until you 'feel better.' It can't be your thinking that's wrong, it must be your body, so change your body." That would be ridiculous. That would be abusive. That would be medical malpractice and criminal.

But this is exactly what our culture has done to trans-men and trans-women. Transgenderism is dysphoria. It is wrong thinking. *In fact, what we now call "Gender Dysphoria" was classified as "Gender Identity Disorder" in the Diagnostic and Statistical Manual of Mental Disorders, Fourth Edition (DSM-IV) until 2013, when it was made to comply with this current wave of political correctness. Until then, it was a disorder. It was known as wrong thinking. But now, it's no longer the thinking that is wrong, it's the body.[6]

The greatest tragedy in this movement is a phenomenon known as Rapid-Onset Gender Dysphoria. It is a form of gender dysphoria that appears suddenly, during or after puberty, in adolescents who show no signs of gender dysphoria in childhood.[7] Although this is not a "medical diagnosis" (at least not yet), it is becoming common to naïve, impressionable youngsters who are immersed in a culture that promotes and celebrates transgenderism. These children, who are emotionally vulnerable and feel uncomfortable with themselves, are strongly influenced by their peers, by the media, and especially YouTube video blogs of trans people who promote the trans lifestyle as the solution to their insecurities. Add to that the "encouragement" of authority figures, such as teachers, doctors, and counselors who are quick to affirm their "felt" gender, and these young people begin to wonder if they too have been misgendered and need to transition.

If we are truly going to help these tortured souls, we need to start from the ethic of truth. Jesus said, "You shall know the truth and truth shall set you free." If a young person starts questioning who they are (i.e. their gender identity), instead of reinforcing wrong thinking, we should insist that it's not their bodies that are wrong, it's their thinking. More specifically, their physical appearance should not be modified, their thinking should be modified. What they need is cognitive therapy based on truth, not hormone treatment and surgical alterations.

We need to tell that boy who "feels" like a girl, "Well, we know you're a boy, so let's start from there and affirm that. Let's find out why you're struggling with your masculinity." We need to tell the girl who "thinks" she's a boy, "Well, we know you're not a boy, you're a girl. So, let's start there, affirm that truth, and investigate why you're uncomfortable with your femininity. Let's investigate what trauma you've been through and why these thoughts are plaguing your identity and let's treat that."

But instead of doing that, we have bought into this "social media, pop-culture, junk science mentality." We've been hijacked by a militant, politically correct, woke-virtue culture and our children are being victimized. Parents rush their kids to a Pediatric Gender Clinic (there are 50 in the United States), often funded by transgender millionaires with a political agenda. The "wokefully" enlightened clinicians tell them, "We need to give your child some drugs to block their puberty and buy them time to explore their gender. Let's give her feelings a chance to tell us what she wants. Your daughter might really be a boy, or your son could actually be a girl." So, the "doctor" prescribes puberty blockers to eight-year-olds and cross-sexual hormones to thirteen-year-olds and by the time they are fourteen they can get gender affirmation surgery which includes a hysterectomy, double mastectomies, or removal of male organs. This is our culture today. Parents are mutilating their children's God-given identities. It is a tragedy that future generations will look back upon with the extreme condemnation—as they should! We need to wake up! It's not their bodies that need to be corrected, it's their thinking.

TRAIN YOUR CHILD IN
THE WAY HE OR SHE SHOULD GO

The third biblical truth regarding gender identity is found in Proverbs 22:6. Parents have a responsibility to train their children in the way they should go, so that when they are old, they will not depart from it. This includes gender. Parents need to instruct and encourage their children to embrace the gender given to them by God.

Is it true some boys demonstrate feminine characteristics? Sure, but doesn't make them female. Plenty of men are not aggressive or competitive, nor do they demonstrate typical masculine qualities. Some may even have effeminate mannerisms. But that doesn't mean they have women's brains and should change their gender to female.

Is it true some girls don't gravitate toward pretty dresses, nail polish, and dollhouses? Are there some girls who would rather climb trees and play football with the boys? Sure, but hardly does that mean they aren't girls, nor does it mean they are on a "gender spectrum" or have an "opposite-sex brain." That's nonsense.

There is no spectrum of gender. It's what we call personality. Some females are tough and competitive, some males are sensitive and passive. So what? God made them who they are. God gave them personality. Don't listen to the lies of the world or be manipulated by the politically correct thought police. Be a parent, train your child in the way he or she should go, and that means honoring and developing the gender God gave them.

GOD LOVES TRANSGENDER PEOPLE

The fourth and final truth regarding transgenderism is simply this: God loves transgender people. Isaiah 42:3 says, "A bruised reed He will not break, and smoking flax He will not quench." God is a loving and compassionate Father. He sees our brokenness; He understands the chaos and confusion of our minds. He knows the deceitful wickedness of our hearts, but He loves us just the same.

Transgenderism is not an issue to be mocked, ridiculed or treated with contempt. Remember that people who experience gender dysphoria are deeply distressed, even suicidal. Sadly, the world exacerbates this by promoting the nonsense that they have somehow been fitted with the "wrong" body and need drugs or surgery to placate the dysphoria in their minds. It's no wonder that transgender individuals experience higher rates of depression and attempted suicide, even after the "remedies" offered by the world have been applied.

Dr. Ryan Anderson makes this point when he wrote: "Sex 'reassignment' doesn't work. It's impossible to 'reassign' someone's sex physically; and attempting to do so doesn't produce good outcomes psychosocially." He continues: "Follow-up of sex-reassigned people—extending over 30 years (has revealed) 10 to 15 years after surgical reassignment, the suicide rate of those who had undergone sex-reassignment surgery rose to 20 times that of comparable peers."[8]

It's the truth that sets us free. Those with gender dysphoria need to be reassured with the truth of who God made them to be and supported in their quest to resolve that truth with the confusion in their minds. When you encounter one who struggles with their gender identity, show grace and mercy. Avoid arguing which pronouns are appropriate and what their truth should be. Instead, be like Jesus and meet them where they are, in the midst of their brokenness. Jesus stepped into the mess of our humanity and met us in the place of our sin and confusion. Rather than demanding we meet some religious expectations, he reached into our lives, cast out our fear with His perfect love, renewed our minds through the power of His Word and promised to never leave us or forsake us.

This is the truth that sets free, and this is what our transgendered friends need. This is what our world needs. They need to know a God who meets us in our pain and brings healing in the midst of it. He accepts us, just as we are. And because He loves us, He picks up the pieces of our broken lives and patiently restores us to the person He created us to be, in body, soul, spirit, and emotions.

Pressure Points

seven
SPEAK THE TRUTH, EVEN IF YOUR VOICE SHAKES

The simple step of a courageous individual is not to take part in the lie. One word of truth outweighs the world.
- Aleksandr Solzhenitsyn

If the world hates you,
know that it hated Me before it hated you.
- John 15:18

The world is in desperate need of Christian preachers and Christian artists and Christian celebrities who put biblical truth before their personal brand. Christians who have achieved prominence and fame must remember that "to whom much is given, from him much will be required" (Luke 12:48). Those who have been given a voice, a platform, or an opportunity to speak, should be careful not to squander their influence on book promotions and public relations intended to bolster their own image. For the Christ follower, platforms should be used to declare the truths Christ has called us to live. In the words of Maggie Kuhn: "Speak the truth, even if your voice shakes."

"But I'm not a pastor or a preacher!" is what some may claim to justify their lack of conviction on cultural strongholds. It's a poor excuse. If you follow Christ, you have a cross to bear, a truth to speak, and a God to glorify. Don't use Christ to promote yourself and advance your brand. The gospel is not a product to be marketed, it is a message to be proclaimed.

What is required today is a generation of prophets who are unafraid and unashamed to speak truth to culture. They may be prophets in the marketplace, pop media or church pulpits—but they are prophets none-the-less. Of course, their truth must be tempered with mercy and love, but it can never be compromised by silence or intimidated by the false gods of tolerance and acceptance. We need an army of leaders who would rather be truthful than trendy, and prophetic than popular.

This is not a plea for the church to become "political." It is a plea for the church to be honest; more specifically, to speak the truth when circumstances call for it. An issue becomes "political" when politicians, pop culture and media are driving a certain narrative about that issue that bolsters their agenda. The church's role in society is to be salt and light. It's not about being political—it's about speaking truth to culture, especially when culture is driving a narrative that is delusional and destructive.

This is when prophets rise. It's not in response to politics. It's in response to culture and the strongholds that imprison it. Prophets speak on behalf of truth. They speak on behalf of God—and what is needed today is a church with a prophetic voice that exposes the lies.

Having said that, it is equally important to discern which issues require a response and which issues do not. Discernment and wisdom are needed. There are times when the church undermines its own credibility by meddling in issues that are better left to the politicians and pundits. Proverbs 26:17 provides an important warning: "He who passes by and meddles in a quarrel not his own Is like one who takes a dog by the ears." We need to learn which dogs to fight and which dogs to pass by.

It is my belief that there are at least three conditions under which the church should speak: (1) when destructive evils become cultural norms; (2) when rebellious leaders flaunt their depravity; and (3) when proposed legislation defies biblical morality. By contrast, there are at least three conditions when the church should not speak: (1) when issues exceed the scope of biblical morality or scriptural mandate; (2) when our actions tether us to certain candidates or political parties; and (3) when the church is being used as a prop to bolster a political agenda or political personality. I am sure this list is not exhaustive, and readers may add better criteria, but may the following provide us with a framework with which to begin.

WHEN THE CHURCH SHOULD SPEAK

When destructive evils become cultural norms.

Several years ago, I attended a pastors' forum addressing the topic of "church and culture." Just previous to that event, in June of 2015, the U.S. Supreme Court struck down all state bans on same-sex marriage, legalized it in all fifty states, and required states to honor out-of-state same-sex marriage licenses. It was a "hot topic" which generated the obvious question, "How should we as pastors respond to this? What should we say to our congregations, if anything at all?" One of the panelists, a senior minister, responded: "I feel no obligation to address this at all in my church. This is not a gospel issue."

I was appalled. Not only was I shocked by this leader's response, but I was also shocked by so many others who fell in agreement behind him. It gave me the impression that many were not thinking on their own; rather, they were looking for someone else to think for them.

Later I addressed this with our pastoral team who attended the event and I stated rhetorically: "How can we not respond to this redefining of biblical marriage? Aren't our people in need of teaching? Should they not hear, from their pastors, what the Bible says about such a serious issue? Won't our people be encountering this question in their schools and places of work; and shouldn't they be equipped with a biblical framework from which to reason and respond?" And then I added, "What about culture? Are we not salt and light? Do we not have a voice in our day, should we not be a prophetic influence? Or do we surrender the public forum to those who simply won a vote? Will that not lead to our being further marginalized and labeled as irrelevant or just plain ignorant? Is this how the decline of the church in society begins?" It wasn't until a few days later that I was greatly encouraged by a public statement issued by the former Assemblies of God General Superintendent, Dr. George Wood who publicly voiced his disagreement over the court's approval of same-sex marriage. It was his statement that I read aloud to our congregation the following Sunday.

One cannot read the scriptures without encountering numerous examples of the faithful confronting evil in culture. Moses challenged Pharaoh's enslavement of the Israelites. Elijah exposed the corruption of King Ahab. Prophets like Isaiah, Jeremiah and Malachi rebuked the immorality and injustice of their days. God's people have always been a trumpet call against toxic culture—it's why Jesus likened us to salt and light. Even beyond biblical times, men like William Wilberforce, Dietrich Bonhoeffer, and Martin Luther King Jr. raised their voices to decry injustices against the poor and the outcast, against women and children and the forgotten of society.

Whenever evil gains a stronghold in society and immorality becomes normal, destruction ensues. Some groups of people will be oppressed, mistreated or suffer in some heinous way. Often, those being abused will be unable to speak for themselves or may be so deceived by the evil afflicting them that they cannot even recognize how they are being maltreated.

Abortion is one such evil in our day. Literally millions of unborn human lives have been violently massacred at the abortion altars of selfish expediency. Who will speak for those who have no voice, if not the church? Yes, we should pray and petition God, but we should also be a light in our world, exposing the atrocities of this murderous industry. Transgenderism is another such evil. It presents itself as a compassionate movement seeking to right those wronged by an "oppressively misgendering culture." Children are encouraged to experiment with gender as doctors prescribe puberty blockers, mandate kids to transgender counseling and even provide them with surgeries to alter their sexuality. This is not compassion, this is insanity. Children need to be instructed and trained about gender, not further confused by culture warriors who manipulate them to advance their own political agendas. If not the church, who will champion the truth about sexual identity to this generation? Who will remind them that we are created by God, in His image, either male or female—that there are two genders, not sixty-seven, determined at birth by chromosomes, not feelings or emotions?

More can be said and has been said in this book about the ruin of marriage and family, the advance of the homosexual agenda, the rise of promiscuity and cohabitation, and the effects of these on society, but the point is clear. When destructive evils become cultural norms, the church needs to be a voice of truth and reason. From the days of Isaiah to the times of Martin Luther King Jr., the world needs to hear from the people of God who bring a message of hope, sanity, and truth to make right the destructive lies of the world.

When rebellious leaders flaunt their depravity.

The church should be known for its willingness to "speak truth to power." It's a familiar phrase that originated in the 1955 pamphlet: *Speak Truth to Power: a Quaker Search for an Alternative to Violence.*[1] From that beginning, influential figures such as Nelson Mandela, Mahatma Gandhi, and Elie Wiesel either demonstrated or advocated the need for truth to be spoken clearly and decisively to leaders. By contrast, Noam Chomsky was dismissive of "speaking truth to power" when he wrote: "Power knows the truth already and is busy concealing it." He believed "the oppressed" needed to hear the truth so they could resist the lies propagated by those in authority.[2] Either way, the church should be known for its clear annunciation of truth and principle.

Jesus called John the Baptist the greatest prophet ever born among women. Yet John worked no miracles. There is no biblical record of him healing the sick or raising the dead. He did, however, raise an entire generation from its spiritual death—not through the laying on of hands—but by preaching truth. His was known as a "baptism of repentance." He confronted the cultural issues of his day and called people to repent. He spoke to local leaders who disobeyed God's laws. He rebuked injustices carried out by soldiers and tax collectors. He even publicly rebuked King Herod for an adulterous affair with his brother, Philip's, wife, and lost his head for it. Indeed, John the Baptist was martyred because he defended the biblical definition of marriage and made no apologies for doing so.

Macaiah was a prophet who lived during the reign of King Ahab in Israel. Ahab was known for surrounding himself with prophetic sycophants who only complimented the king and encouraged him to do whatever was in his heart (1 Kings 22:6). During a visit from King Jehoshaphat of Judah, the neighboring king discerned that these prophets had no credibility due to their unwillingness to "speak truth to power." Jehoshaphat asked, "Is there not a prophet of the Lord here?" In other words, "Is there no one here who can rightly discern the Word of God and declare it with clarity and precision?" King Ahab answered, "There is one man, Micaiah the son of Imlah… but I hate him, because he does not prophesy good concerning me, but evil."

Macaiah was known for his willingness to speak truth to Ahab. He wasn't interested in being the king's friend or enjoying the privileges that came with access to power; he cared only about one thing: "What does God want me to speak?" This was especially important in the presence of so many who refused to speak it. In fact, Micaiah accused all the other prophets in the king's court of being controlled by lying spirits—a remark that resulted in him being physically assaulted. This was not a man who cared about making friends, being accepted, or maintaining his popularity. He cared only about speaking truth and exposing lies.

Now is not the time for muddled responses and vague explanations that safeguard one's popularity. Now is not the time to squander our influence on building a social media presence or earning a "blue check mark" on Twitter. This generation needs leadership: a clear and decisive response to the issues of the day. Politicians and pop stars are ripping our culture apart and deceiving millions into an eternity without Christ. These are not people we should be embracing as friends in the public forum, these are false prophets we should be exposing as enemies of the public good.

When proposed legislation defies biblical morality.

In January 2019, The New York State Legislature adopted the

Reproductive Health Act (RHA) into law. The RHA was significant because it expanded abortion rights and eliminated important restrictions on abortion in the state. Prior to the passage of the RHA, New York banned third-trimester abortions (except to save the life of the mother) and required that abortions be performed by only licensed physicians. The RHA legalized abortion whenever "necessary to protect a woman's life or health." This opens the door to a very liberal rationalization for abortion under ambiguous criteria. Furthermore, the RHA allows health care practitioners, other than licensed physicians, to perform abortions; this means abortion on demand is readily available to any who want it while diminishing standards for safety and health. Also under the RHA, murder of the unborn is removed from the criminal code. If a fetus dies as the result of an assault against a pregnant woman there would be no prosecution because the unborn child is no longer recognized as a legitimate human being with rights.

As horrible as all this may be, perhaps even more tragic is what occurred upon passage of the RHA. The moment it passed, the state legislature celebrated with standing ovation and shouts of joy, followed by dressing the Empire State Building in pink lights—the color of the abortion advocacy group, Planned Parenthood.

This is not political. This is immoral. This is an evil act that directly violates God's command, "Thou shalt not kill." It cheapens the sanctity of life and is the rotten fruit of a culture lost to its own narcissism and self-indulgence. There is no other explanation for a society that legalizes, with cheerful exuberance, the intent to murder tens of thousands, even millions of its own unborn children. A gruesome darkness has taken hold of our national soul and the church (as salt and light) should rise with a united call to repentance.

Is this too harsh? Does this sound angry? Perhaps it is, but is there not a cause? At the time of this writing, according to the Centers for Disease Control, one out of every three unborn babies in New York City is murdered within its mother's womb.[3] One out of three! And according to New York State's legislative leadership, that's not enough. More blood must be offered on the altars of our indulgence. With this new legislation, the number of abortions will skyrocket in New York to unbelievable heights. Heaven weeps. Hell rejoices. And the church must speak!

If you think this is too strong, educate yourself. Read the medical description of a late-term abortion procedure. Learn the true demographics of those mothers subjecting their unborn to these horrors. Rarely does it involve the physical health of the mother. Realize the violent means by which these children are carved from the womb. It is a violent and depraved act. The Lozier Institute describes it as follows:

> Abortions performed after 20 weeks gestation, when not done by induction of labor (which leads to fetal death due to prematurity), are most commonly performed by dilation and evacuation (D & E) procedures. These particularly gruesome surgical techniques involve crushing, dismemberment and removal of a fetal body from a woman's uterus, mere weeks before, or even after, the fetus reaches a developmental age of potential viability outside the mother.[4]

What are we to do? Weep! Weep and repent, and plea to God for His mercy as Jeremiah did for his nation and Daniel did for his people in captivity. Speak out as Isaiah did. Declare the truth as Macaiah did. Teach your people as the Apostle Paul did. Oppose abortion and the politicians who support it. This is what the church does. Yes, we preach the gospel; yes, we make disciples—but we also influence culture. We act as salt and light in the world, restraining evil from advancing its strongholds on the hearts and minds of men.

What about the "Separation of Church and State?"

On October 7, 1801, the Danbury Baptist Association of Danbury Connecticut wrote to Thomas Jefferson expressing concern over religious freedom. It was a concern born from the persecution they were suffering because of their refusal to join a certain religious establishment. Jefferson responded to their concerns in a letter dated January 1, 1802. It is from this letter we take the phrase "Separation of Church and State." The text in part is as follows:

> Believing with you that religion is a matter which lies solely between man and his God; that he owes account to none other for his faith or his worship; that the legislative powers of the government reach actions only, and not opinions, I contemplate with sovereign reverence that act of the whole American people which declared that their legislature should 'make no law respecting an establishment of religion, or prohibiting the free exercise thereof,' **thus building a wall of separation between church and State**. Adhering to this expression of the supreme will of the nation in behalf of the rights of conscience, I shall see with sincere satisfaction the progress of those sentiments which tend to restore man to all of his natural rights, convinced he has no natural right in opposition to his social duties.

The doctrine of "Separation of Church and State" is a cardinal American truth, but unfortunately, it is largely misunderstood and misconstrued by those who resent any involvement of religious people. Jefferson's argument was not that the church or church leaders should be prohibited from influencing the state, his position was that the state should be prohibited from controlling the church. His statement is supposed to prevent the government from interfering with how people worship; it is not to prevent religious people from advocating for or against certain political issues. In fact, our own Pledge of Allegiance states "One nation, under God, indivisible. With liberty and justice for all." In other words, our nation is supposed to be indivisible (or inseparable) from God.

While it is true that the church should not be political, it is also true that it is the freedom of every citizen (including church leaders) to express their opinions and be involved in politics as they see fit. The danger is when we tie the church as a corporate entity, or our ministry purpose, to political causes. The church should not become mired in partisan political matters; it should, however, guide its members—and society as a whole—toward biblical principles and encourage Christians to vote for those who are aligned with biblical truth.

WHEN THE CHURCH SHOULD NOT SPEAK

When issues exceed the scope of biblical morality or the church's scriptural mandate.

There will always be issues that provoke emotional reactions, especially from Christians concerned about morality. However, we would be wise to avoid debates that stray from biblical absolutes into political opinions. In other words, when certain issues do not correlate to specific scriptural judgments, the church should refrain from becoming dogmatic defenders of a politician's policy or a political platform. Individuals need the humility to recognize their strong opinions can often be informed more from personal experience and political preference rather than Bible truth. We should avoid tethering the church to a political view when that view is not strictly biblical.

The church is not a political body. Although "evangelicals" are often calculated as a voting bloc, we who are evangelicals understand that politics is always a far second to God's Word. Our concern should not be with politics, but with issues. We have no loyalty to the republicans, democrats or any other group; our loyalty is to the Lord Jesus Christ and the truths of His Word. Candidates or platforms that violate biblical morality, promote injustice or enable corruption should be resisted, ardently, by the followers of Christ.

In Luke 12:13-14, Jesus was asked to adjudicate a specific issue. A man from the crowd said, "Teacher, tell my brother to divide the inheritance with me." Jesus replied, "Man, who made Me a judge or an arbitrator over you?" Clearly, Jesus could have addressed the matter; He is the Judge of all the earth and had the capacity to administer justice. However, Jesus understood the scope of His mission was not to advocate for earthly reform. He didn't come as courtroom judge, to become mired in social arguments. He came as Savior to die on the cross and restore mankind to fellowship with God. Accordingly, He turned the conversation into a sermon on greed and how covetousness distracts people from salvation. This is further indicated when His followers tried to "take Him by force to make Him king" (John 6:15). Jesus refused the coronation, knowing this was not His mission. Other examples are seen in the apostles who rarely addressed the evils of the Roman Empire but instead focused on preaching the gospel and establishing churches.

Indeed, there will be issues that Christians must address—especially when those issues are malignant evils corrupting society and darkening men's hearts. However, we must be careful not to mistake our mission to be that of social justice concerns, political interests or moralism. In doing so, we risk tethering the church to causes outside the scope of our primary purpose: winning the lost and being a light for Christ in this world.

When our actions tether us to politicians or political parties.

A recent report from an Evangelical Leaders Survey revealed that nearly 90 percent of evangelical leaders do not think pastors should endorse politicians from the pulpit. Leith Anderson, president of the National Association of Evangelicals (NAE) stated, "Evangelicals emphasize evangelism, and pastors often avoid controversies that might take priority over the gospel message."[5]

Indeed, the pulpit should be a place for preaching the gospel and making disciples, not for promoting political views. George Wood, former Superintendent of the Assemblies of God said, "Our focus should be on the gospel. If we begin to endorse candidates, then we are politicizing the Church, diluting our message, and bringing unnecessary division among our people. It is sufficient that we can speak on issues without endorsing specific candidates for office."[6]

Pastors may certainly speak out on specific cultural issues, especially when the Bible provides guidance on those issues. In fact, most pastors believe they have a responsibility to present biblical clarity on cultural matters. But they also believe it is essential to avoid endorsement of a particular politician or political party. In fact, federal law prohibits churches (as tax-exempt entities) to "participate in or intervene in any political campaign on behalf of (or in opposition to) any candidate for public office."[7] This prohibition comes from legislation known as the "Johnson Amendment" developed by Senator Lyndon B. Johnson in 1954. An article in *Influence Magazine* further clarifies:

> While the Johnson Amendment applies to churches whose pastor makes public statements from the pulpit or in church publications in favor of or in opposition to political candidates, the IRS says that it does not apply to political statements by pastors off of church property and not in official church publications so long as they are accompanied by a statement that the comments are strictly personal and not intended to represent the church. The Johnson Amendment only applies to intervention in political campaigns. It does not apply to efforts to influence legislation. Section 501(c)(3) of the tax code bars exempt organizations from engaging in "substantial" efforts to influence legislation. But unlike the complete bar to campaign intervention, the ban on attempts to influence legislation only pertains to substantial efforts. Exempt organizations, including churches, that violate these limitations risk losing their tax-exempt status as well as the ability of donors to make tax-deductible donations to them.[8]

When the church is being used as a prop to bolster a political agenda or political personality.

The story is told of an eighteenth-century evangelist named Peter Cartwright who was known for his uncompromised preaching. One day, the President of the United States, Andrew Jackson, came to Cartwright's church. Knowing their pastor's tendency to preach boldly, the elders warned Cartwright not to offend the president for fear of retribution against their church or denomination. When the young preacher came to the pulpit he said, "I understand that President Andrew Jackson is here this morning. I have been requested to be very guarded in my remarks lest I offend him.

Therefore, allow me to address this at the onset: if Andrew Jackson does not repent of his sin, he will go to an eternal hell just like any sinner!" The entire congregation gasped with shock; the church elders almost fainted. How dare this preacher publicly offend the President of the United States? Following the service, everyone wondered how President Jackson would respond to Cartwright when meeting him at door. The president looked him sternly in the eye and said, "Sir, I wish I had a regiment of men with the boldness you've shown. I could conquer the world!"[9]

Indeed, politicians would love to have pastors and churches endorse them. In fact, many will court church leaders attempting to garner their support. However, Christian leaders today need to be cautious and deliberate when given access to political power. We must guard ourselves from being enamored by personalities and stay on mission. Our call is not to make friends with presidents and kings, our mission is to speak truth—especially to those in high office. Furthermore, we must take heed of connecting ourselves to politicians whose primary concerns are winning elections. By doing so, we tether our integrity to theirs and give them power over credibility—or at least the public's perception of it. Paul said church leaders should remain "above reproach." Our public reputations should not be tethered to politicians who often compromise their convictions for political expedience. In fact, when an opportunity presents itself, preachers should speak out against rulers who mock God or sin openly lest their example has the effect of normalizing immorality. Of course, this should be done with respect and high esteem for the office, but it should be done none-the-less.

This does not mean pastors or churches should refrain from praying for, interacting with, or offering biblical guidance to political leaders. In fact, the church is under a scriptural mandate to do so. In 1 Timothy 2:1-3, Paul instructs Timothy, "Therefore I exhort first of all that supplications, prayers, intercessions, and giving of thanks be made for all men, for kings and all who are in authority, that we may lead a quiet and peaceable life in all godliness and reverence. For this is good and acceptable in the sight of God our Savior."

While praying for and advising civic authorities, church leaders should ensure that their interaction is entirely non-partisan. This means that pastors and churches should regularly pray for and provide biblical guidance to leaders regardless of their political persuasion or positions on issues. We should intercede for them, speak to them and influence them no matter who they are, how they legislate or what party they belong to. In so doing, the church maintains an objective posture and remains nonpartisan when it comes to personalities and politics but stays loyal to the scripture's command to pray for "all" who are in authority.

Clearly, we need discernment when interacting with political figures. Many in elected positions are not above "using" a pastor's visit to bolster his or her image with constituents. Not only could this diminish the pastor's credibility, but it can also become a source of division in the body. Therefore, if one is called upon to pray for or visit a political leader, and that interaction is going to be publicized, or possibly used as a political prop, the pastor should make a statement of his or her own. Using social media, email, or some vehicle to communicate publicly, announce your intended visit ahead of time, make it clear that your attendance should not be misconstrued as an endorsement or alignment, but is an opportunity to fulfill a biblical mandate to pray for those in government. Further, it is important to state that this type of visit would occur regardless of who the leader may be, or what political party they may represent.

Remember the prophets who often met with government officials: Macaiah, Elijah, Isaiah, Jeremiah, and Daniel. They did so without endorsing them and often made clear their positions on issues from a prophetic or biblical perspective. While you may not have the chance to prophesy to a leader or be asked to share your biblical views, you can do so in other formats—while respecting and honoring the offices of those involved.

As we engage culture, let us be careful not to become political hacks or pawns of a party narrative. A political hack is a pejorative describing someone who acts only in the best interest of the political party to which he or she is loyal. To a political hack, truth does not matter, nor do the principles involved. The only concern is the party narrative. A political hack ignores obvious lapses in truth or integrity when it serves the narrative and often manipulates facts to promote the interests of the party.

Pastors should never become hacks who are loyal to parties and personalities. Our loyalty is to Jesus Christ and His Word. Our call is to lead people out of darkness, into truth and into a relationship with Jesus Christ. When we speak, it is never to promote a political position, it is to reveal truth—to preach the gospel. Sometimes that truth will align with a political goal, sometimes it will not. But such alignment is of no consequence. We speak to point people toward Christ, whether it serves a political end or not.

Pressure Points

eight

A CALL FOR COMPASSIONATE CONFRONTATION

Those around us—especially the lost and broken—must always know that we see them as God's creations, having infinite, immeasurable value. The way we speak to them, the tone we use, and the words we choose must communicate a sincere empathy and concern for their lives, their families, their health and their hurting souls.

My prayer is that *Pressure Points* has not only renewed your spirit with a passion for truth but has also provoked you to speak that truth when opportunities arise. In doing so however, I wish to offer a caution. We must remember that our calling is not to win arguments or defend personal standards of morality. Our calling is to transform lives through the power of the gospel. This means our words must not only be full of truth, but also of grace and wisdom. Proverbs 11:30 says "He who wins souls is wise." There must be an excellence to our spirit and a quality to our character that reflects the love of God, the wisdom of His Word and sincerity of our concern for the souls of men.

To do this, our words must demonstrate compassion. There is a familiar quote often attributed to Plato: "Be kind; everyone you meet is fighting a hard battle." Compassion is the ability to recognize suffering in others. It understands that people with confused morals are often acting out of wounded, broken souls. They may have made bad choices and are suffering the consequences, but compassion realizes that there are forces beyond their understanding, compelling them to act in destructive ways.

This is one reason why Ephesians 4:32 tells us to "Be kind and compassionate to one another…just as in Christ, God forgave you" (NIV). God has compassion on us because He understands how broken and corrupt we truly are. He knows we are driven by a sinful nature that lacks the capacity to be good. Therefore, He has compassion on us just as we should have compassion on others. Rather than criticizing someone's lifestyle, we should treat lost people with mercy and kindness, realizing that they are victims of a broken nature.

Our words must convey respect. While speaking about transgender issues at Stanford University, political commentator Ben Shapiro stated: "If I were in a room with a transgender person, having dinner with that person I wouldn't go out of my way to call them by their biological sex. It is rude. I wouldn't do that if I were sitting right across from them. But if you're asking me in a public forum whether a man is a man or a woman is a woman, or you're asking me to call a man a woman or a woman a man, the answer is no."[1]

In other words, in the context of personal relationship and private conversation, it is entirely appropriate to refer to someone by their preferred pronouns. It is a sign of respect toward that person and tolerance for the choices they have made even though you may disagree with them. It demonstrates that you regard that person enough to preserve the relationship by appreciating their sensibilities. Confronting their delusion will only result in offense and anger and convince them that you really do not care.

The same applies to those in same-sex marriages or even cohabiting relationships. Acknowledging that one's same sex partner is his "husband" or her "wife" or affirming that one's live in boyfriend is his or her "partner" is not an immoral act on your part. It is simply a private affirmation that these are the choices made by autonomous individuals. You may disagree with them, but such are the realities of their lives to which they are now entitled by law.

The difference however, as Ben Shapiro states, is in a public forum. When an individual (especially a leader) is addressing these issues publicly—perhaps from the pulpit, in a panel discussion, or in a media interview—there is a responsibility to speak truth to culture and influence the multitudes who are listening. In this context, pastors and spiritual leaders should not worry about who might be offended when speaking the truth; instead, they should worry about who will continue being deceived if they do not. This means if we are asked if a biological man can become a woman, or if same-sex marriage is outside of God's plan, or if cohabitation is sin, or abortion is murder, we should be clear and unambiguous. Culture needs to hear truth, not comforting, politically correct niceties lacking in clarity.

Our words must communicate patience. The Bible calls it "longsuffering." More specifically, 1 Corinthians 13:4 says "Love suffers long and is kind." Patience is the ability to tolerate someone even when you disapprove of his or her lifestyle. Patience is the parent who doesn't reject a son or daughter because of his or her sinful conduct, because that parent believes God is not willing that any should perish and is drawing that prodigal back to Himself. Patience is the deacon who welcomes an unusual visitor who is flagrantly transitioning his or her gender, because that deacon believes God wants to heal that person's pain and brokenness. Patience is the pastor who is gentle and calm with angry, rebellious souls that mock and ridicule the gospel, because that pastor believes the Holy Spirit is convicting and convincing them toward salvation.

Our words must be firm. In demonstrating patience, we must be careful not to become "enablers." Enabling is a term often used to describe people who empower others to persist in self destructive behavior (such as substance abuse or alcoholism). An enabler will remove the consequences of a person's bad choices or provide excuses for unhealthy lifestyles which make it possible for the person to persist in their own destruction.

Ambivalence or ambiguity toward those who persist in sin only enables them to continue in it. If we avoid warning them of sin's consequence, we are enabling them. If we imply, even tacitly, that God will forgive them and accept them without repentance and conversion, we are enabling them. If we appear to be at peace with their sin and express an approving attitude toward it, we are complicit in their deception. Therefore, we need to be firm in our declaration of truth and not waiver in the face of resistance.

Most of all, our words must reveal our love. Jesus said, "By this all will know that you are My disciples, if you have love for one another" (John 13:35). Most people expect to be judged and condemned for their sin. They believe Christians will look down on them and reject them because of their lifestyles. But those around us—especially the lost and broken—must always know that we see them as God's creations, having infinite, immeasurable value. The way we speak to them, the tone we use, and the words we choose must communicate a sincere empathy and concern for their lives, their families, their health and their hurting souls. They must see in us—and feel from us—the love of Jesus Christ, who went to the cross to take their sin, absorb God's wrath, redeem their souls and save them from eternal death.

Demonstrating love, however, does not mean that we avoid the difficult conversations. It is because we love them that we tell them the truth. It is because we care about our families and friends that we warn them of sin's consequences and refuse to participate in it. We forbid it in our presence. We remove the provisions that facilitate it and absence ourselves from situations where they commit it or ceremonies that celebrate it. It is a difficult tension, but it is possible. Be patient with people, affirm your love for them, but always oppose the behavior that is destroying their lives and condemning their souls to an eternity without Christ.

Showing love by speaking truth is especially relevant to spiritual leaders. The nature of pastoring involves a million difficult conversations. There will be times when cohabiting individuals will apply for active membership in the church or someone in a homosexual relationship will ask to be water baptized. There will be church members who dabble in adultery and women contemplating abortions. In these instances, to love them is to speak the truth. Pastors and church leaders must have the difficult conversations about lifestyle choices, willful sin, and the biblical requirement of repentance followed by submission to the Lordship of Jesus Christ. Failing to do so gives unregenerate parishioners a false hope and enables them to persist in their sin.

May God help us to engage our families, friends, neighbors

and parishioners. May He empower us to speak the truth with love, compassion, wisdom and grace.

Pressure Points

INTRODUCTION TO APPENDICES

Since the earliest days of Christianity, the church has had conflicts with surrounding culture. This is especially true when society's norms threatened to take root in the church and its leaders were forced to respond. Such encounters occurred in the New Testament and continued as the church expanded through history.

In 21st century American culture, these challenges continue. While there is concern over the broad spectrum of immorality in society, specific issues have emerged as pressure points for the church: abortion, same-sex marriage, transgenderism, cohabitation, moral relativism and atheistic evolution. Sadly, many believers, churches and denominations have acquiesced to these pressures and embraced them in defiance of scripture. The culture of this world is taking root in the church and soon the two will be indistinguishable.

Concerned that this trend shows no signs of abating, I initiated an effort in the church I pastor to affirm our biblically held positions and declare our fidelity to the canon of scripture as it relates to these pressure points. This is crucial, especially as the church grows and more people join as members. Failing to address these issues proactively could result in a future membership populated with individuals who approve of these practices, even tacitly. The outcome could be a next-generation of voting members that may resist, or even oppose future attempts to affirm sincerely held biblical beliefs.

The first step in this process was to address my concern with our leadership team. Before speaking to these issues publicly, it was important to unite our leaders in this effort and prepare them in the event there were questions from our congregation. As well, I wanted to give them an opportunity to provide feedback and speak into this process. Their wisdom was a great benefit and helped me to approach this initiative with both sensitivity and boldness.

The next step was to teach our people. To do this we launched an eight-week series entitled "Worldview." It addressed each of the pressure points listed in this book from a biblical perspective and helped our people to formulate proper apologetics from God's Word. In fact, each chapter of *Pressure Points* represents a sermon that was delivered from the pulpit on Sunday Mornings.

Once the series concluded, we implemented the final step: presenting a resolution to our membership to update our constitution and bylaws. Not only was it important to teach our people biblical truths regarding these pressure points, it was essential that we empower our church as a religious not-for-profit corporation against potential legal attacks on our religious beliefs. More often we are witnessing how society forces churches to perform unbiblical marriages, hire individuals who practice sinful lifestyles or use religious facilities in ways that violate biblical principles. We must be prepared.

In the pages that follow, I have provided two appendices. The first is a sample introduction to a resolution on marriage, sexuality and sanctity of life and the second is the actual resolution. These are templates based upon what was adopted in our church. If you intend on using them in your situation, please be sure to consult an attorney or contact Alliance Defending Freedom (ADF). Certain state laws or restrictions may apply, and these documents should not be used without consulting legal advice.

APPENDIX I

INTRODUCTION TO RESOLUTION: MARRIAGE, SEXUALITY AND SANCTITY OF LIFE

In order to preserve the function and integrity of (name of church) as the local Body of Christ, and to provide a biblical role model to (name of church) members and the community, it is imperative that all persons who become members in (name of church), or who are employed, or who serve as volunteers, agree to and abide by the following standards contained in this Statement on Marriage, Sexuality and Sanctity of Life (Matt 5:16; Phil 2:14-16; 1 Thess. 5:22).

In defining (name of church)'s position on these issues and certain behaviors defined as sin in God's Word, it should be noted that God offers redemption and restoration to all who confess and forsake their sin, seeking His mercy and forgiveness through Jesus Christ. (Acts 3:19-21; Rom 10:9-10; 1 Cor 6:9-11). We believe that every person is created in God's image and must be afforded compassion, love, kindness, respect, and dignity. (Mark 12:28-31; Luke 6:31.) Hateful, disrespectful or harassing behavior or attitudes directed toward any individual are to be repudiated and are not in accord with Scripture nor the doctrines and practices of (name of church).

The Bible teaches that God wonderfully and immutably created humankind in His image: male (man) and female (woman), sexually different but with equal personal dignity. These two distinct, complementary genders together reflect the image and nature of God (Gen 1:26-27). Rejection of one's biological sex is a rejection of the image of God within that person; therefore, we agree with the dignity of individual persons affirming their biological sex. Further, we denounce any and all attempts of individuals to physically change, alter, or disagree with their predominant biological sex—including but not limited to elective sex-reassignment, transvestite, transgender, or non-binary "genderqueer" acts or conduct.

The Bible teaches that the term "marriage" has only one meaning: the uniting of one biological man and one biological woman in a single, exclusive union, as delineated in Scripture (Gen 2:18-25). The Bible further teaches that God intends sexual intimacy to occur only between a man and a woman who are married to each other (1 Cor 6:18; 7:2-5; Heb 13:4). The Bible also teaches that God has commanded that no intimate sexual activity be engaged in outside of a marriage between a man and a woman. We, therefore, believe that cohabitation, or "living together" without the formal union of marriage between a man and a woman, violates God's principle of marriage, promotes promiscuity, and undermines the biblical definition of family.

The Bible teaches that any form of sexual immorality (including adultery, fornication, homosexual behavior, bisexual conduct, bestiality, incest, and use of pornography) is sinful and offensive to God (Matt 15:18-20; 1 Cor 6:9-10). We further believe that homosexuality or sexual relations between individuals of the same sex is strictly prohibited by Scripture and identified as sin against the laws of God and a departure from the biblically defined nature of sexuality (Leviticus 18:22; 20:13; Romans 1:25-27; 1 Timothy 1:9,10).

The Bible teaches the sanctity of human life. Scripture reveals that life begins at conception and that every unborn human life is a special creation of God with purpose and destiny (Luke 1:31, 36; Job 31:15; Is. 44:2, 24; Ps. 139:13-16; Jer. 1:5; Luke 1:11-17, 41, 44). Accordingly, we believe that terminating a pregnancy constitutes the murder of human life and scripture is explicit concerning the taking of innocent human life. "You shall not murder" (Ex. 20:13) is a moral imperative that recurs throughout Scripture (cf. Mat. 19:18, Rms. 13:9).

APPENDIX II

RESOLUTION ON MARRIAGE, SEXUALITY AND SANCTITY OF LIFE

1. WHEREAS, since the earliest days of Christianity, church leaders addressed theological challenges, sinful practices and immoral cultural standards that threatened to take root in the church; and,

2. WHEREAS, the church today is under similar pressure from worldly culture to accept as normal what the Bible clearly identifies as sinful and immoral; and,

3. WHEREAS, the issues of homosexuality, same-sex marriage, transgenderism, cohabitation, and abortion have emerged as predominate cultural issues the church is facing; and,

4. WHEREAS, these practices, which are clearly defined in scripture as sinful behaviors that violate God's laws, have brought controversy to the church as society is pressuring the church to accept and approve these practices; and,

5. WHEREAS, many believers, churches and denominations have acquiesced to these pressures and have embraced these practices in defiance of scripture; and,

6. WHEREAS, many Christians are losing their ability to discern the dangers of accepting these practices as appropriate behaviors for Christ-followers; and,

7. WHEREAS, it is likely that many newcomers seeking membership in (name of church) may not be clear on the biblical standards regarding homosexuality, same-sex marriage, transgenderism, cohabitation, and abortion, which may result in a future membership populated with individuals who approve of these practices; and,

8 WHEREAS, the leadership of (name of church) believes it has become necessary for the church to identify and address these issues from a biblical perspective; and,

9 WHEREAS, it is more prudent to identify and address the biblical perspective on these issues now rather than later, as debate on these issues is likely to become more hostile and spirited as time progresses; therefore, be it

10 RESOLVED, that (name of church) membership adopt the following statement on Marriage, Sexuality and Sanctity of Life into (name of church)'s Constitution as Article -- ; and, be it further

11 RESOLVED, that all subsequent Articles in the Constitution be renumbered in proper sequence following Article --.

12 ARTICLE – (NAME OF CHURCH) STATEMENT ON MARRIAGE, SEXUALITY AND SANCTITY OF LIFE

13 In order to preserve the function and integrity of (name of church) as the local Body of Christ, and to provide a biblical role model to (name of church) members and the community, it is imperative that all persons who become members in (name of church), or who are employed, or who serve as volunteers, agree to and abide by the following standards contained in this Statement on Marriage, Sexuality and Sanctity of Life (Matt 5:16; Phil 2:14-16; 1 Thess. 5:22).

14 In defining (name of church)'s position on these sincerely held religious beliefs and certain behaviors defined as sin in God's Word, it should be noted that God offers redemption and restoration to all who confess and forsake their sin, seeking His mercy and forgiveness through Jesus Christ (Acts 3:19-21; Rom 10:9-10; 1 Cor 6:9-11). We believe that every person is created in God's image and must be afforded compassion, love, kindness, respect, and dignity (Mark 12:28-31; Luke 6:31). Hateful, disrespectful or harassing behavior or attitudes directed toward any individual are to be repudiated and are not

in accord with Scripture nor the doctrines and practices of (name of church).

15 The Bible teaches that God wonderfully and immutably created humankind in His image: male (man) and female (woman), sexually different but with equal personal dignity. These two distinct, complementary sexes together reflect the image and nature of God (Gen 1:26-27). Rejection of one's biological sex is a rejection of the image of God within that person; therefore, we agree with the dignity of individual persons affirming their biological sex. Further, we denounce any and all attempts of individuals to physically change, alter, or disagree with their predominant biological sex—including but not limited to elective sex-reassignment, transvestite, transgender, or non-binary "genderqueer" acts or conduct.

16 The Bible teaches that the term "marriage" has only one meaning: the uniting of one biological man and one biological woman in a single, exclusive union, as delineated in Scripture (Gen 2:18-25). The Bible further teaches that God intends sexual intimacy to occur only between a man and a woman who are married to each other (1 Cor 6:18; 7:2-5; Heb 13:4). The Bible also teaches that God has commanded that no intimate sexual activity be engaged in outside of a marriage between a man and a woman. We, therefore, believe that cohabitation, or "living together" without the formal union of marriage between a man and a woman, violates God's principle of marriage, promotes promiscuity, and undermines the biblical definition of family.

17 The Bible teaches that any form of sexual immorality (including adultery, fornication, homosexual behavior, bisexual conduct, bestiality, incest, and use of pornography) is sinful and offensive to God (Matt 15:18-20; 1 Cor 6:9-10). We further believe that homosexuality or sexual relations between individuals of the same sex is strictly prohibited by Scripture and identified as sin against the laws of God and a departure from the biblically defined nature of sexuality (Leviticus

18:22; 20:13; Romans 1:25-27; 1 Timothy 1:9,10).

18 The Bible teaches the sanctity of human life. Scripture reveals that life begins at conception and that every unborn human life is a special creation of God with purpose and destiny (Luke 1:31, 36; Job 31:15; Is. 44:2, 24; Ps. 139:13-16; Jer. 1:5; Luke 1:11-17, 41, 44). Accordingly, we believe that terminating a pregnancy constitutes the murder of human life and scripture is explicit concerning the taking of innocent human life. "You shall not murder" (Ex. 20:13) is a moral imperative that recurs throughout Scripture (cf. Mat. 19:18, Rms. 13:9).

Pressure Points

ENDNOTES

Introduction
1. Colson, Charles W., *How Now Shall We Live* (Carol Stream Illinois, Tyndale House Publishers, 1999), x
2. https://www.pewforum.org/fact-sheet/changing-attitudes-on-gay-marriage/

Chapter One
1. Kellar, Timothy, *Shaped by the Gospel*, (Grand Rapids MI, Zondervan Publishers, 2016), 22
2. https://www.gotquestions.org/sola-scriptura.html
3. https://www.outreach.com/print/article.aspx?article_name=a-messagetitles

Chapter Two
1. Orwell, George. Nineteen Eighty-Four. (First published in England 1949 by Martin Secker and Warburgh Limited)
2. ACLU Tweet; 2:46 PM, Nov 19, 2019
3. http://penelope.uchicago.edu/Thayer/E/Roman/Texts/Herodotus/3a*.html#38
4. Patterson, James, The Day America Told the Truth, (Plume, 1991)
5. Kouchaki, M., Smith-Crowe, K., Brief, A. P., & Sousa, C. (2013). *Seeing Green: Mere exposure to money triggers a business decision frame and unethical outcomes. Organizational Behavior and Human Decision Processes*
6. https://www.foxnews.com/opinion/why-are-so-many-christians-biblically-illiterate
7. https://www.christianitytoday.com/edstetzer/2015/july/epidemic-of-bible-illiteracy-in-our-churches.html
8. ibid
9. https://www.barna.com/research/millennials-oppose-evangelism/
10. https://albertmohler.com/2016/01/20/the-scandal-of-biblical-illiteracy-its-our-problem-4/

Chapter Three
1. https://www.huffpost.com/entry/12-famous-scientists-on-the-possibility-of-god_n_56afa292e4b057d7d7c7a1e5
2. https://www.pbs.org/wgbh/questionofgod/voices/collins.html
3. https://en.wikipedia.org/wiki/List_of_Christians_in_science_and_technology
4. Huse, Scott M., *The Collapse of Evolution*, (Grand Rapids MI., Baker Books); 3
5. Colson, Charles W., *How Now Shall We Live* (Carol Stream Illinois, Tyndale House Publishers, 1999), 66
6. https://www.asa3.org/ASA/education/origins/nabt.htm
7. ibid
8. See Kitzmiller v. Dover Area School District (4:04-cv-02688) District Court, M.D. Pennsylvania
9. Berlinski, David, *The Devil's Delusion: Atheism and its Scientific Pretensions*, (New York NY, Basic Books)
10. Crick, Francis, *Life Itself* (New York NY, Simon and Schuster,1981) 51-52.
11. Fred Hoyle, *The Intelligent Universe* (Holt Rinehart & Winston; 1st edition 1983), 11
12. https://www.cnsnews.com/blog/michael-w-chapman/ben-carson-it-takes-lot-more-faith-believe-evolution-believe-god-evolution

Chapter Four
1. Bonow, Amelia; Nokes, Emily, *Shout Your Abortion*, (Oakland, CA, PM Press, 2018)
2. https://www.nationalreview.com/news/women-defy-shoutyourabortion-with-their-stories-of-regret/
3. https://silentnomoreawareness.org/rc/testimony.aspx?id=2857
4. https://www.nationalreview.com/news/women-defy-shoutyourabortion-with-their-stories-of-regret/
5. Fienberg, John S., Fienberg Paul D., *Ethics for a Brave New World Second Edition* (Wheaton Illinois, Crossway) 2010
6. See info at https://www.guttmacher.org/united-states/abortion
7. ibid
8. https://abort73.com/abortion_facts/states/new_york/
9. https://www.governor.ny.gov/news/governor-cuomo-signs-legislation-protecting-womens-reproductive-rights
10. https://www.usatoday.com/story/opinion/2019/02/05/ralph-northam-advocating-abortion-infanticide-worse-than-blackface-column/2776498002/
11. Washington Examiner, May 07, 2019 (online article)
12. O'Rahilly, Ronand; Muller, Pabiola, *Human Embryology and Teratology*, 2nd ed. (New York: Wiley-Liss, 1996) 8, 29
13. Singer, Peter, *Practical Ethics, 2nd Edition*. (Cambridge: Cambridge University Press, 1993) 85-86
14. Fridhandler, Louis, "Gametogenesis to Implantation," *Biology of Gestation, vol. 1*. (Elsevier Inc., 1968) 76
15. Moore, Keith L., *The Developing Human: Clinically Oriented Embryology*. 2d ed. (Philadelphia PA, Saunders, 2013). 1

16. Gilbert, Scott F., *Developmental Biology*; Chapter 4: Fertilization: Beginning of a New Organism, (MA, Sunderland: Sinauer Associates; 2000)
17. Potter, E. L.; Craig, J. M., *Pathology of the Fetus and the Infant, 3d ed.* (Sedalia, MO, Year Book Medical Publishers, 1975) Vii
18. Subcommittee Report on Separation of Powers to Senate Judiciary Committee S-158, 97th Congress, 1st Session 1981.
19. https://www.congress.gov/bill/106th-congress/house-bill/4888
20. https://www.youtube.com/watch?v=wOlFEJbRIeo&t=1693s
21. Wolf, Naomi; "Our Bodies, Our Souls," The New Republic, October 16, 1995, 26
22. Paglia, Camille; "Fresh Blood for the Vampire," Salon, September 10, 2008
23. Livingstone-Smith, David; *Less Than Human: Why We Demean, Enslave and Exterminate Others*, (Spokane Valley, WA, Griffin Publishing, 2012)
24. https://nrlc.org/uploads/factsheets/FS01AbortionintheUS.pdf
25. Alcorn, Randy. *Pro-Life Answers to Pro-Choice Arguments.* (Colorado Springs, CO. Multnomah Books)

Chapter Five
1. https://www.guttmacher.org/fact-sheet/american-teens-sexual-and-reproductive-health
2. https://www.webmd.com/sex-relationships/news/20061220/premarital-sex-the-norm-in-america researchers
3. Twenge, Jean M.; Sherman, Ryne A.; Wells, Brooke E. "Changes in American Adults' Sexual Behavior and Attitudes,1972–2012," Archives of Sexual Behavior, May 2015. doi: 10.1007/s10508-015-0540-2.
4. https://issuu.com/relevantmagazine/docs/sept_oct_2011
5. https://www.patheos.com/blogs/revangelical/2014/05/26/rethinking-sex.html
6. https://www.match.com/dnws/cp.aspx?cpp=/cppp/magazine/article0.html&articleid=12437
7. Some Patterns of Non-exclusive Sexual Relations Among Unmarried Cohabiting Couples; Cunningham, Antill and Huang; pgs.265-274
8. Jarvie, Jenny. Institute for the Study of Civil Society; "Unmarried Couples 'More Likely to Cheat'; The Telegraph. www.telegraph.co.uk
9. Treas, J; Giesen, D; The Family in America; "Sexual Infidelity Among Married and Cohabiting Americans," Journal of Marriage and the Family; pgs.48-60
10. Stanton, Glen; *Why Marriage Matters;* (Colorado Springs CO. 1997) 57
11. "The Role of Cohabitation in Declining Rates of Marriage"; Journal of Marriage and Family; pg. 913-927
12. See information at www.skepticsstackexchange.com

Chapter Six
1. https://leginfo.legislature.ca.gov/faces/billTextClient.xhtml?bill_id=201920200ACR99
2. "Sexual Orientation & Homosexuality"; American Psychological Association; Aug. 30, 2017
3. "Sexuality and Gender: Findings from the Biological, Psychological, and Social Science"; The New Atlantis; Fall 2016 - Lawrence S. Mayer, MD, PhD; Paul R. McHugh, MD
4. "On the Causes of Homosexuality"; Statement of National Association for Research and Therapy of Homosexuality; Aug. 31, 2017
5. "Transgenderism: A Pathogenic Meme"; June 10, 2015, Mchugh, Paul; see article at https://www.thepublicdiscourse.com/2015/06/15145/
6. *Diagnostic and Statistical Manual of Mental Disorders, Fourth Edition,* Text Revision. Copyright 2000 American Psychiatric Association
7. If you need guidance in dealing with Rapid-Onset Gender Dysphoria, visit https://www.parentsofrogdkids.com/
8. Anderson, Ryan T. *When Harry Became Sally,* (New York NY, Encounter Books, 2018)

Chapter Seven
1. American Friends Service Committee, *Speak Truth to Power: A Quaker Search for an Alternative to Violence,* (American Friends Service Committee)
2. See article: "Noam Chomsky: Speaking Truth to Power" at https://chomsky.info/20100803
3. https://www.cdc.gov/mmwr/volumes/67/ss/ss6713a1.htm
4. https://lozierinstitute.org/the-reality-of-late-term-abortion-procedures
5. https://www.nae.net/pastors-shouldnt-endorse-politicians
6. Ibid
7. see 26 U.S.C. §501(c)(3)
8. https://influencemagazine.com/Practice/Should-Pastors-Endorse-Politicians-From-the-Pulpit This article originally appeared in the September/October 2018 edition of Influence magazine
9. https://christianhistoryinstitute.org/it-happened-today/9/25

Chapter Eight
1. https://www.youtube.com/watch?v=4IgzE1-dt3c

ABOUT THE AUTHOR

Gregg Johnson is Lead Pastor of The Mission Church where he has served for over thirty years. Known for its emphasis on foreign missions, community outreach, leadership development and discipleship programs, The Mission Church is a vibrant, growing church making an impact for Jesus Christ both locally and internationally.

Ordained with the Assemblies of God, Pastor Gregg also serves as Executive Presbyter for the Eastern Region of the Assemblies of God New York Ministry Network. In that capacity, he acts as leadership coach and consultant to the various pastors and leadership teams in the Eastern Region of New York State

Gregg Johnson is also founder and keynote speaker of Global Leadership Training providing ministry coaching, study materials and leadership training conferences to church, civic and corporate leaders throughout East and West Africa, India, Cuba, Canada and the United States. He has conducted over 50 conferences worldwide which have been endorsed and attended by respected leaders such as the President and Vice President of Ghana, the Chief Justice of the Supreme Court of Ghana and the Mayor of Kigali, Rwanda, Administrative Governor of Kampala, Uganda as well as Assemblies of God General Superintendents of Ghana, Kenya, Tanzania, Malawi, Rwanda, Zambia, Cuba and other denominational leaders.

Pastor Gregg Johnson has authored nine books on leadership and personal development including, *Pressure Points, Upward: Taking Your Life to the Next Level, Leading from the Second Chair, How the Mighty Have Fallen, The Trust of Leadership, The Character of Leadership, Raising the Standard of Leadership, Ethics for Church Leaders*, and *Conflict, Crisis and Change*.

Pastor Gregg and his wife, Laura, live in New York. They have five adult children and four grandchildren.

For more information visit
www.GreggTJohnson.com